Vegan, vegetarian and pescetarian nutrition

Oliver Rumle Hovmand

Disclaimer: This book has been thoroughly researched, but the opinions offered herein is only for educational and entertainment purposes only. Before making any changes, readers should consult a health professional such as a physician or a nutritionist. The author and the publisher have made a great effort to ensure that the accuracy and completeness of the information contained in this book, but we assume no responsibility for errors, inaccuracies, omissions, or any inconsistency herein.

Oliver would like to thank two of his parents, his mom and his Jens for letting him stay with them while he worked on this and more interesting projects. He would also like to thank authors and other people who have written about this subject, and who might have provided inspiration, and have made information available. All vegans and vegetarians of the West are still pioneers, and the more we can talk and write about our habits of eating, the better for ourself, our unborn children, the animals, the environment etc. Someday we might just change the world, you know.

© 2010 Oliver Rumle Hovmand and Ohbsessed
Text, cover design and interior design by Oliver Rumle Hovmand
1st edition
Printed and distributed by Lightningsource
ISBN: 978-87-993883-1-8

Ohbsessed
Vindebækvej 14
4792 Askeby
Denmark
CVR-nummer: 32802850
www.ohbsessed.com

Vegan, vegetarian and pescetarian nutrition

Oliver Rumle Hovmand

Ohbsessed publishing
- International division

Intro

People decide to go vegetarian, pescetarian or vegan for a large variety of reasons. Common reasons are environmental, care for animals, realisation of how the Western diet is destroying the health of the Western world, economic reasons, belief in nonviolence and for religious reasons. A great deal of studies has shown that animal products are serious health hazards, making vegetarians and especially vegans much less liable to suffer heart disease, cancer, diabetes, osteoporosis, and beside of this are very few vegans and vegetarians overweight or obese. Vegetarians and vegans do not consume the drugs given to keep animals alive until they are slaughtered, consume dramatically fewer pesticides than do meat eaters, and do also consume much fewer heavy metals like mercury, than do meat eaters. Nor do they ingest the germs latent in dead animals, and they will not have meat starting to rot while passing thru the intestine of the human body, measuring more than eight meters, and with a temperature similar to the rest of the body.

Three kinds of plant-based diets
Individuals consuming a plant-based diet is divided into a large number of groups. The three most common groups are vegetarian, vegan and pescetarian.

Pescetarians are individuals that do not eat meat from animals that lives on land, but eat animals from the sea like fish and shellfish. Pescetarians eat fish, eggs, dairy products and all fruit, nuts, grains, beans and other kinds of plants. The word, pescetarian is a combination of the Italian word pesce that means fish, and the English word vegetarian. Many pescetarins have the goal to become a vegetarian or a vegan, and only uses the pescetarian diet in the process of transition, from the Western diet to a fully plant-based diet. For others it is simply just the middle ground between eating the Western diet and eating a vegetarian or vegan diet. Some pescetarians describes themselves as vegetarians and many omnivores consider pescetarians as vegetarians, but that is clearly wrong since fish and seafood are not vegetables.

Vegetarians are individuals that only eats bi-products of animals. They eat dairy products, eggs, grains, nuts, fruit, beans and other plants. Vegetarians are divided into three subgroups. Ovo-lacto vegetarians eat both eggs, dairy products and plants. Ovo vegetarians eat eggs and plants, but do not eat dairy products. Lacto vegetarians do not eat eggs, but do eat dairy products and plants.

Vegans does not use animal products of any kinds. This both includes eggs, dairy products, leather, silk, wool, E-numbers containing animal products and what could else be thought of as an animal product.

Raw vegans follows a vegan diet, but does only eat plants that are not cooked.

Fruitarians follows a vegan diet, but does only consume plants that can be gathered and harvested without harming the plant.

Plant-based diets are perfectly safe.
Dietic associations and states around the worlds affirms and acknowledges that both vegan, vegetarian and pescetarian diets can meet all known nutrient needs, and be just as healthy as mainstream omnivorous diets. And just like omnivorous diets, plant-based diets needs to include a vide variety of foods like vegetables, fruits, grain products, seeds, leafy green vegetables and legumes.

The American Dietetic Association fully acknowledges that vegan, vegetarian and pescetarian diets can meet all needs. In a paper, they write:
"It is the position of the American Dietetic Association that appropriately planned vegetarian diets, including total vegetarian or

vegan diets, are healthful, nutritionally adequate, and may provide health benefits in the prevention and treatment of certain diseases. Well-planned vegetarian diets are appropriate for individuals during all stages of the life cycle, including pregnancy, lactation, infancy, childhood, and adolescence, and for athletes."

It's easy
Changing your diet to a pescetarian, vegetarian or vegan diet is as hard as you choose to make it. It is all up to your self whether you want to make a big deal out of it, or keep it mellow and just act as nothing special happened. But truth be told, something very special happens and you will sure thing not regret it. Some go vegetarian, pescetarian or vegan overnight and others choose to gradually decrease the amount of the animal product they want to stop with before making the change to a vegan, vegetarian or pescetarian diet.

Many people go thru all three stages of plantdom, starting out as a pescetarian. Many pescetarian do then after a period of time come to the conclusion that they no longer will eat meat, and decide to become vegetarian. Many people starts as a vegetarian, and do then over time realise that it is not very smart to eat animal products and end up on the last mainstream step of plantdom: veganism.

Other books on the subject have tended to mainly cover the subject from an American perspective, and have not taken into account that veg-friendly products is not available in many countries. I have tried to write in a way that makes the information useable for people living in whatever country the book is accessible in.

Simply put: This books aim to cover what you would need to know on all three stages of plantdom, meaning that you will not have to buy a new book or learn new things when or if you decide to take your habits of eating plants to the next level. I, Oliver H. hope that it can be of use to you. If it turns out that way, so have I been happy to help.

Protein

Vegans, vegetarians and pescetarians should not worry anymore about getting enough protein than omnivores. Omnivores should not worry, so vegans, vegetarians and pescetarians should be home free. But most people think that you can not have a too high intake of protein and that protein can only be an advantage.

This school of thought comes from several hundred years ago, the 18th century, where doctors thought that if individuals with enough money to obtain as much meat they wanted to have a high intake of protein, they would do so by instinct and would naturally be making the right decision by doing so. Later on workers and soldiers of Europe and the US were studied and a recommended daily intake of 189 gram protein was made. Some time after the recommendations were changed on account of animal experiment. A study conducted in 1913 showed that rats fed animal protein such as meat and dairy grew faster than rats fed plant protein. This led to the hailing of eggs, meat and dairy as "Class A protein," and vegetable protein to be labeled as "Class B" protein. The team of researchers conducting the experiment, just forgot to take into account, that many kinds of animal products like milk is stuffed with growth hormones, and that rats is not humans and have some decidedly different needs than humans because they simply have to grow faster than humans.

In 1903, the head of Yale's department of biochemistry released a study showing significant health benefits of cutting back on protein. The recommendation of that time recommended 150 gram protein daily, but the team of researchers conducting the study recommended a daily intake of only 50 gram. In the 1940-ties, another study showed that the lover limit of human protein intake was placed at 20 gram protein daily. The study also showed that all of the essential amino acids scientists of earlier times have doubted was found in plants, was found in plants.

The study even found that all of the essential amino acids needed for survival and well being, was found in all kinds of starches and vegetables.

Many populations of the world have worked hard and prospered on one type of vegetable alone. People living in the rural areas of Poland in the 1900-hundred have fed on a diet consisting almost only of potatoes with no problems obtaining micronutrients or macronutrients. Lag of protein is almost unknown. The hungry children of the poor African countries shown in the news once in a while suffers from an overall lag of calories. Because as soon as these humans gets access to their normal starch and vegetable based diet again, they begin to thrive, and gain weight and muscle again. Even though humans that have starved for a long time, needs more protein than people who had have access to food all the time, because they need to rebuild what they lost during the time of starvation, do humans that die from starvation die because of a lag of fat, and not a lag of protein. The body looses all of its fat, but large amounts of its protein remain when they are dead.

You will get enough protein
For some reason have the population of the Western world come to think that it is hard to get enough protein, and that protein is only found in a few select types of food. This concern about protein is highly misplaced, because even though protein is an vital and necessary nutrient, the body does not need a huge amount of it as many people think.

Mainstream sources suggest that ten percent of the daily calories should come from protein, so one calorie should come from protein, when ten is eaten. 0.8 grams of protein should be eaten per kilogram you weigh, which is about 0.36 grams protein per pound you weigh. This recommendation includes a wide safety margin, but just to be perfectly safe, and because some plant proteins are digested different than plant protein, 1 gram protein per kilogram body weight should work even in a worst case scenario, or 0.45 gram protein per pound of body weight. A general rule of thumb is that if you eat enough calories, and eat a well balanced diet consisting of a vide variety of foods, you will get enough protein. Ofcourse, fruits, fats, alcohol and sugars do not contain much protein, but if you eat a diet of sweet alcohol shots, oil and bananas you will also find it difficult to get enough vitamins.

Plants and meat contains about the same protein.
A common myth is that animal source protein is better than vegetable source protein. This is just a downright lie, or a myth if you will. The protein found in meat, eggs, dairy and plants are all build of amino acids. The body does not require protein, but it needs what protein is build of: the amino acids. The body needs 20 common amino acids, but it is unable to make nine of those amino acids by itself. Therefore, those nine amino acids must be obtained from dietary sources. And without those nine amino acids, the body is simply not able to make protein. But luckily all of the essential amino acids is found in vegetable protein, and as long as you get enough protein, should not need to worry.

Vitamins

The diet is the source of many important nutrients needed by the body, and low intake of specific nutrients can cause certain diseases. In older times, nineteenth century physiologist perceived food and diets to be sources of only five types of nutrients: protein, fat, water and ash which was meant as the residue from combustion, which is minerals. These five types of nutrients accounted for almost 100 percent of the mass of most foods. But research and important discoveries in the fields of microbiology caused a shift in paradigm, and the vital nutrients today called vitamins were discovered.

The name, "vitamine" was coined by a Polish biochemist named Casimir Funk. He eluded the nature of what would later be called thiamine or Vitamin B1, and discovered that thiamine was a molecule of such importance that it was a "vital amine," and suggested the term "vitamine" as a name for what today is defined as vitamins.

A vitamin is defined as an organic compound distinct from fats, carbohydrates and proteins. It is a natural component of foods, where it is usually present in minute amounts, and it is essential to maintain normal physiologically functions like growing, maintenance, development and production. Its absence and underutilization causes a specific deficiency syndrome, and it is not synthesized in amounts adequate to meet the needs, in the body of those who needs it. The definition of vitamins has its limitations, especially to the last part of the definition. Because many animal species, humans too can synthesize some of the vitamins. Humans can for an example synthesize Vitamin D when they are exposed to sunlight, which for humans spending most of their time outside makes Vitamin D more a hormone than a vitamin.

13 substances or groups of substances are currently recognized as being vitamins by the scientific community as a whole, and others are

proposed as being vitamins too. Most vitamins come in different forms called vitamers. Vitamin A do for an example have three vitamers which all can be used as Vitamin A by the body, called Retinol, Retinal and Retinoic Acid. Vitamin A do also have so called provitamins, which is carterenoids that can be metabolised to yield the metabolic active form of Vitamin A.

Antioxidants
Vegetables, fruits and other plant products are the best source of antioxidants. And excessive consumption of foods rich in antioxidants is one of the reasons why vegetarians tends to live 10 years longer than meat eaters, and vegans often lives 15 years longer than meat eaters. Antioxidants such as Vitamin C, Vitamin E and Vitamin A, and minerals like selenium and zinc prevent beneficial substances and organs in the body from becoming oxidated. In the body, oxidation takes place. This is a vital process, but it creates free radicals which is atoms, molekules, or ions with unpaired electrons. These substances want to pair up with another substances and destroy it, making chain reactions happens that creates yet more free radicals. Free radicals reacts with the body's DNA, cell membranes proteins etc. The Free radicals are created by fat, stress, cigarette smoke and pollution from cars and factories. Antioxidants works to reduce oxidate damage and is linked to prevent a significant amounts of diseases like cancer and heart disease.

But as with many other things, too much of a good thing can also be harmful in this case. Studies have showed that too high intake of some substances like Vitamin C can hurt the health of the body instead of improving it.

Vitamin D
Adults need about 15 micrograms of Vitamin D daily. Individuals older than 50 years of age should consume 10 micrograms daily, and those older than 75 years should consume 15 micrograms daily.

The tolerable upper intake level of Vitamin D is 50 micrograms daily. Vitamin D is both a hormone and a vitamin. Vitamin D can both be synthesized in the skin like a hormone, and be obtained from dietary sources like a vitamin. Many individuals meet their Vitamin D needs through exposure to sunlight. A dietary source of Vitamin D is needed for people living northern countries like Greenland, Sweden and northern state of the US. Here, individuals tend not to get enough sunlight, why dietary sources of Vitamin D are needed. Studies have showed that the UV energy above 42 degrees northern latitude, which is a line approximately between the northern border of California and Boston is insufficient for vitamin D synthesis in the skin from November through February and in far northern latitudes, this reduced intensity lasts for up to 6 months. In the United States, latitudes below 34 degrees north (a line between Los Angeles and Columbia, South Carolina) allow for cutaneous production of vitamin D throughout the year.

Vegan dietary sources of Vitamin D includes fortified foods and supplements. In the United Kingdom, Canada, United Kingdom and other countries soy milk and cereals are fortified with Vitamin D. But in other countries such as Denmark fortification of consumer products is illegal, making supplements the only dietary source of Vitamin D. Vegetarian dietary sources of Vitamin D is milk, eggs and dairy products.

Two kinds of Vitamin D can be obtained from dietary sources and be used in the body: D2 from plant origin and D3 from animal origin.

Vitamin D is essential to keep calcium in the blood at a sufficient level, obtain calcium from dietary sources and maintain or improve the health of the bones. Vitamin D is synthesised in the skin. When ultraviolet light from the sun hits the skin, it converts cutaneous 7-dehydrocholesterol to previtamin D3, which in turns becomes Vitamin D3, which is one of the types of Vitamin D the body can use. Individuals with white or light skin are better at producing Vitamin D. The daily doses needed, can be produced by only 10 to 15 minutes of sunlight on an area corresponding in size to the forearms and face. People with darker skin require about three to six times longer time in the sun to produce a daily dose of Vitamin D. The larger area of the skin that is covered by clothing or other things, the longer time does it take to produce Vitamin D.

When Vitamin D is synthtized in amounts larger than we need does it gets stored in the body for times where production of Vitamin D in the skin is low. Older individuals produce smaller amounts of Vitamin D, and is mostly only capable of producing half as much Vitamin D as young individuals. Sunscreen makes the body produce significantly lower amounts of Vitamin D, and some studies suggest that production of Vitamin D is lowered by 70 percent when sunscreen is used. The sunlight of the whole day can be used to produce Vitamin D, and the light provided by dedicated sunlamps can also be used to synthesize Vitamin D.

Vitamin A and Beta-Carotene
Adults need 900 micrograms of Vitamin A daily. The tolerable upper intake level of Vitamin A is 3000 micrograms.

Vitamin A is found in vegan sources such as carrots, broccoli, potatoes, kale, spinach, pumpkin, apricot, papaya, mango, peas, tomatoes, nectarine, papaya, seaweed, cantaloupe, peppers, turnip etc. Vegetarian sources are milk and eggs, and pescetarian sources are fish.
Vitamin A is essential for eye health, for maintaining and growing the bones and the teeth, and plays vital parts in the immune system.

Vitamin C
Adults need 90 milligrams of Vitamin C daily. Individuals who smoke should consume slightly more, and are suggested to add about 35 milli-

grams. The tolerable upper intake level of Vitamin C is 2000 milligrams.

Vitamin C is also called Ascorbic Acid. Vegan sources of Vitamin C are grape, gooseberry, pepper, kiwifruits, broccoli, elderberry, tomato, potato, strawberry, cabbage, leafy green vegetables, mango, lime, passion fruit, oranges etc. Vegetarian sources of Vitamin C are eggs and dairy products.
Vitamin C is needed by the body in order to build blood vessels and bones, to resist infections, to absorb iron etc. Studies show that vegans and vegetarians have higher levels of Vitamin C than do meat-eaters, and are much more likely to meet the estimated daily requirements.

Vitamin E
Adults need 15 milligrams of Vitamin E daily. The tolerable upper intake level of Vitamin E is 1000 milligrams.

Vitamin E is also called d-Alpha Tocopherol. Vegan sources of Vitamin E are nuts, seeds, leafy green vegetables, seaweed, whole grain, wheat germ, olive oil, sunflower oil etc. Vegetarian sources of Vitamin E are dairy and egg products. Pescetarian sources are fish.
Vitamin E is needed to stabilize cell membranes and to prevent oxidation. Most individuals consume only about half of the Vitamin E needed, but vegans and vegetarians will logically consume more Vitamin E. It might be a good idea to take supplements of Vitamin E.

Vitamin K
Adults need 80 microgram of Vitamin K daily.

Vegan sources of Vitamin K are broccoli, leafy green vegetables, cabbage, asparagus, lentils, peas, seaweed, soybeans, kale, pumpkin etc. Vegetarian sources are milsk and dairy products, and pescetarian sources are fish. Vitamin K plays a part in regulation of calcium in the blood and helps with blood clotting. Vitamin K intake among meat-eaters tend to be four or five times the estimated daily requirement. Vegans and vegetarians will logically consume even more Vitamin K.

The B Vitamins

There are eight B Vitamins which all plays essential parts in cell metabolism. They are all needed in order to make dietary sources of energy such as fat, protein and carbohydrates into energy useable by the body. All beside of one, Vitamin B12 is present in vegetables sources today, but due to changes in the farming industry, Vitamin B12 can only be obtained from supplements and fortified food on a vegan diet, and thru eggs and dairy on a vegetarian diet. The B-vitamins, except for B12 tend to be found in types of plants such as legumes, grains, seeds, nuts, green vegetables, and in nutritional yeast and yeast used for fermentation.

Daily recommended allowance tends to be quite low for all of the B-vitamins, and all can without problem be obtained from a vegan or vegetarian, except for Vitamin B12 which is not found in the agricultural produce of today. Often will the vegan and vegetarian diet provide larger amounts of Vitamin B, then do most omnivorous diets.

Vitamin B1

Adults needs 1.2 milligram Vitamin B1 daily.

Vitamin B1 is called Thiamin and it is found in vegan sources such as nuts, grains, yeast, seeds, kale, asparagus, flax, cauliflower, potatoes and oranges. Vegetarian sources of Vitamin B1 is eggs and dairy products.

Vitamin B1 helps convert carbohydrates to energy, plays a part in amino acid metabolism and are a key ingredient in the well being of the nervous system. Well balanced vegan and vegetarian diets contains large amounts of Vitamin B1, and vegans do not need to worry.

Vitamin B2
Adults need **1.3 milligram Vitamin B2** daily.

Vitamin B2 is called Riboflavin and it is found in vegan sources such as mushrooms, leafy green vegetables, fortified cereals and soymilk, asparagus, peas, almonds, bananas, legumes, potatoes and grains. Most studies shows that vegans and vegetarians gets adequate amounts of Riboflavin.

Vitamin B3
Adults need **16 milligram Vitamin B3** daily. The tolerable upper intake level of Vitamin B3 is 35 milligrams.

Vitamin B3 is called Niacin and it is found in vegan sources such as grains, nutritional yeast, legumes, vegetables, fruits, leafy green vegetables, seeds and starch, mushrooms. Vegetarian sources of Vitamin B3 are dairy products and eggs, and pescetarian sources are fish.
The liver can synthesize Vitamin B3 from the amino acid tryphotan which is found in all plant protein. Studies have shown that vegan and vegetarian diets contains plentiful Vitamin B3.

Vitamin B5
Adults need **5 milligram Vitamin B5** daily.

Vitamin B5 is called Pantothenic Acid and it is found in all plant foods such as grains and vegetables. Vegetarian sources of Vitamin B5 are dairy and egg products.
Since all plants contains Vitamin B5, all studies have showed that vegan and vegetarian diets supply sufficient amounts of Vitamin B5.

Vitamin B6
Adults need **1.3 milligram Vitamin B6** daily. Individuals older than 50 years should consume 1.7 milligram daily. The tolerable upper intake

level of Vitamin A is 100 milligram.

Vitamin B6 is called Pyriodoxine and it is found in vegan sources such as nutritional yeast, grains, legumes, soy products, seeds, peas, potatoes, watermelon, squash, asparagus, seaweed, bananas, figs, elderberries, tomatoes, oranges, etc. Vegetarian sources includes milk and eggs. Studies have found that vegans and vegetarians gets plenty of Vitamin B6.

Vitamin B7
Adults need **30 micrograms Vitamin B7** daily.

Vitamin B7 is also called Biotin. Vegan sources of Vitamin B7 are vegetables, soybeans, grains, legumes, seeds, nuts.
Studies have showed that vegans and vegetarian consumes more Vitamin B7 than do omniwhores.

Vitamin B9
Adults need **400 micrograms Vitamin B9** daily. The tolerable upper intake level of Vitamin A is 1000 micrograms.

Vitamin B9 is also called folate and folic acid. Vegan sources of Vitamin B9 are asparaguses, leafy green vegetables, broccoli, avocado, corn, beets, oranges, bananas, grapefruits, seeds, grains, squash, cauliflower, cantaloupe, strawberries, sesama tahini, peanuts etc.
Studies have shown that vegans and vegetarian consumes more Vitamin B9 than omniwhores do.

Vitamin B12
Adults needs **2.4 micrograms Vitamin B12** daily. If you are pregnant, thinking about becoming pregnant or if you are lactating you should consume 2.8 micrograms daily.
Vitamin B12 is among other names also called cobalamin and it is not

found in any plant products that we know of, why vegans and vegetarians are recommended to eat supplements or foods that are "fortified" or "enriched" to get the recommended daily allowance. Several types of soymilk, cereal, tofu, tempeh and nutritional yeast are fortified, but in some countries like Denmark, Europe fortification of groceries is illegal, making supplements like multivitamin the only way secure way of getting enough Vitamin B12. All people older than age 50 is also recommended getting large parts of their B12 intake as supplements of fortified foods because they loose the ability to absorb Vitamin B12 in its protein-bound form.

The body needs vitamin B12 for cell division, blood formation, building of DNA, protection of nerve fibers and other important functions.Vitamin B12 is made by bacteria and fungi. Several decades ago, back when farms weren't factories and a guy named Old McDonald actually could be found working in the field or petting the pigs, Vitamin B12 could be obtained from the starches and vegetables found in the diet. Back then, a greater amount of fungi and bacteria was found in the diet, and these bacteria would contribute to more B12 in vegetables. But today, when we eat potatoes they are cleaned to perfection and are grown in bad soil treated with all kinds of toxins. This means that vegetables and fruits no longer can be relied on as a source of Vitamin B12, and the only secure way of obtain Vitamin B12 is by eating fortified foods or supplements. Bacteria living in the human large intestine produce Vitamin B12, but studies have showed that the body isnt able to absorb it why it does not help to prevent Vitamin B12 deficiency.

Some vegan propaganda points out that vegans do get enough Vitamin B12 without taking supplements or eating fortified food. This is at the moment not true, and it cannot be recommended to experiment. All vitamins are essential to the body, and Vitamin B12 is not an exception. Vitamin B12 deficiency can cause severe and potential irreversible damage to the brain and nervous system and symptoms of mania and psychosis. Neither animals nor plants can make Vitamin B12, but animals eat food and dirt contaminated with Vitamin B12 and stores it in the body. This Vitamin B12 is consumed by vegetarians thru dairy and eggs, and by omnivores as meat, dairy and eggs. But at great cost to their health, offcourse.

More than 95 percent of the cases of B12-deficiency, is not due to inadequate dietary intake of Vitamin B12. 10 to 30 percent of all individuals older than 50 years lose the ability to absorb B12 in its protein-bound form which is found in animal products. This is due to secretions of gastric acid and the enzyme pepsin in the stomach, but these individuals prospers on the sources of Vitamin B12 found in fortified foods and supplements. Besides, a condition known as pernicious amenia develops in two percent of the elderly population, which causes their stomach to lose the ability to produce a protein used to carry.

Other cases of Vitamin B12 deficiency happen when the body lose the ability to produce the molecule that transports Vitamin B12 around in the body. Vitamin B12 is transported around the body by a molecule called Intrisic Factor. When the body fails to synthesise Intrisic Factor, supplements, animal products or fortified foods is not enough, and Vitamin B12 should be obtained from an injection.

The body recycles Vitamin B12 so that it can use the Vitamin B12 molecules over and over again. Some individuals recycle Vitamin B12 better than others, and some have gone for as long as twenty years without dietary sources of Vitamin B12. Other bodies are less efficient at recycling Vitamin B12, making them run out relatively fast if they do not consume dietary sources of Vitamin B12.

Vitamin content of foods: units per 100 g edible portion

	A (IU)	D (IU)	E (mg)	K (mg)	C (mg)
Cereals					
Barley, cooked	7		0.05	0	0
Bulgur, cooked	0		0.029	0	0
Whole-grain corn flour	469		0.25	0	0
couscous, cooked	0		0.013	0	0
Millet, cooked	0		0.18	0	0
Oat bran, cooked	0		0	0	0
Oats	0		0.7	0	0
Brown rice, cooked	0		0.72	0	0
White rice, cooked	0		0.05	0	0
Wild rice, cooked	0		0.23	0	0
Wheat germ, crude	0		0	0	0
Whole-grain wheat flour	0		1.23	0	0
White wheat flour	0		0.43	0	0
Wheat bran, crude	0		2.32	0	0
Tapioca, pearl, dry	0		0	0	0
Whole-wheat spaghetti	0		0.05	0	0
Spinach spaghetti	152		0	0	0
Spaghetti	0		0.07	0	0
Sorghum	0		0	0	0
Rye flour	0		1.33	0	0
Buckwheat, cooked	0		0.236	0	0
Bread, cakes and pastries					
Bread, cracked-wheat	0		0.564	0	0
Bread, French/Vienna	0		0.236	0	0
Bread, Irish soda	194		1.057	0	0.8
Bread, Italian	0		0.277	0	0
Bread, mixed-grain	0		0.615	0	0.3

Data from The Vitamins, Fundamental Aspects in Nutrition and Health

B1 (mg)	B2 (mg)	B3 (mg)	B6 (mg)	B5 (mg)	Folic acid (µg)	B12 (µg)
0.083	0.062	2.063	0.115	0.135	16	
0.057	0.028	1	0.083	0.344	18	
0.246	0.08	1.9	0.37	0.658	25	
0.063	0.027	0.983	0.051	0.371	15	
0.106	0.082	1.33	0.108	0.171	19	
0.16	0.034	0.144	0.025	0.217	6	
0.763	0.139	0.961	0.119	1.349	56	
0.096	0.025	1.528	0.145	0.285	4	
0.163	0.013	1.476	0.093	0.39	3	
0.052	0.087	1.287	0.135	0.154	26	
1.882	0.499	6.813	1.3	2.257	281	
0.447	0.215	6.365	0.341	1.008	44	
0.189	0.031	1.83	0.084	0.50	18	
0.523	0.577	13.58	1.303	2.181	79	
0.004	0	0	0.008	0.135	4	
0.108	0.045	0.707	0.079	0.419	5	
0.097	0.103	1.53	0.096	0.183	12	
0.04	0.01	0.900	0.01	0.06	2	
0.237	0.142	2.927	0	0	0	
0.287	0.114	1.727	0.268	0.492	19	
0.04	0.039	0.94	0.077	0.359	14	
0.358	0.24	3.671	0.304	0.512	39	
0.52	0.329	4.749	0.043	0.387	31	
0.298	0.269	2.405	0.083	0.25	10	
0.473	0.292	4.381	0.048	0.378	30	
0.407	0.342	4.365	0.333	0.515	48	

	A (IU)	D (IU)	E (mg)	K (mg)	C (mg)
Bread, oat bran	5		0.395	0	0
Bread, oatmeal	16		0343	0	0.4
White pitabread, enriched	0		0.038	0	0
Whole-wheat pitabread	0		0.934	0	0
Bread, pumpernickel	0		0.507	0	0
Bread, raisin	2		0.758	0	0.5
Bread, rye	4		0.552	0	0.2
Bread, wheat bran	0		0.674	0	0
Bread, wheat	0		0.546	0	0
Bread, wheat germ	1		0.87	0	0.3
Bread, white	0		0.286	0	0
Bread, whole-wheat	0		1.036	0	0
Boston cream pie	80		1.064	0	0.1
Fruitcake	78		3.12	0	0.4
Gingerbread	55		1.372	0	0.1
Pound cake	606		0	0	0.1
Cheesecake	552		1.05	0	0.6
Animal crackers	0		1.837	0	0
Brownies	69		2.134	0	0.1
Chocolate chip cookies	3		0	0	0.3
Chocolate sandwich cookies with cream filling	1		3.03	0	0
Fig bars	44		0.702	0	0.02
Fortune cookies	10		0.344	0	0
Gingersnaps	1		1.488	0	0
Graham crackers	0		1.907	0	0
Molasses cookies	1		2.08	0	0
Oatmeal cookies	16		2.822	0	0.4
Peanut butter cookies	29		3.516	0	0
Raisin cookies	41		1.543	0	0.3
Vanilla wafers	1		0	0	0
Cheese crackers	162		1.012	0	0
Matzo crackers	0		0.402	0	0

B1 (mg)	B2 (mg)	B3 (mg)	B6 (mg)	B5 (mg)	Folic acid (µg)	B12 (µg)
0.504	0.346	4.831	0.04	0.159	25	
0.399	0.24	3.136	0.068	0341	27	
0.599	0.327	4.632	0.034	0.397	24	
0.339	0.08	2.84	0.231	0.548	35	
0.327	0.305	3.091	0.126	0.404	34	
0.339	0.398	3.466	0.069	0.387	34	
0.434	0.335	3.805	0.075	0.44	51	
0.397	0.287	4.402	0.176	0.536	25	
0.418	0.28	4.124	0.097	0.436	41	
0.369	0.375	4.498	0.098	0.313	55	
0.472	0.341	3.969	0.064	0.39	34	
0.351	0.205	3.837	0.179	0.552	50	
0.408	0.27	0.191	0.026	0.301	8	
0.05	0.099	0.791	0.046	0.226	3	
0.189	0.186	1.562	0.038	0.224	10	
0.137	0.137	1.311	0.035	0.341	11	
0.028	0.193	0.195	0.052	0.571	15	
0.35	0.326	3.47	0.022	0.376	14	
0.255	0.21	1.721	0.035	0.547	12	
0.289	0.266	2.767	0.262	0.146	6	
0.079	0.179	2.074	0.019	0.172	5	
0.158	0.217	1.874	0.075	0.364	10	
0.182	0.13	1.84	0.013	0.297	10	
0.2	0.293	3.235	0.183	0.339	6	
0.222	0.314	4.122	0.065	0.537	17	
0.355	0.264	3.031	0.241	0.425	7	
0.267	0.23	2.227	0.054	0.207	7	
0.17	0.18	4.27	0.07	0.437	32	
0.216	0.206	1.967	0.054	0.31	9	
0.361	0.209	2.976	0.026	0.526	8	
0.57	0.428	4.671	0.553	0.526	25	
0.403	0.291	3.892	0.115	0.443	14	

	A (IU)	D (IU)	E (mg)	K (mg)	C (mg)
Melba toast crackers	0		0.234	0	0
Rusk toast crackers	46		0	0	0
Rye crackers	0		1.362	0	0
Rye wafers crackers	23		1.999	0	0.1
Saltines crackers	0		1.653	2	0
Wheat crackers	0		4.012	0	0
Butter Croissants	539		0.43	0	0.2
Plain Croissants	0		0	0	0
Danish pastry, cheese	203		2.583	0	0.1
Danish pastry, fruit, enriched	52		1.759	0	3.9
Doughnuts	57		3.457	0	0.2
Doughnuts, glazed	10		0	0	0.1
Blueberry muffins	34		1.049	0	1.1
Blueberry pancakes	199		0	0	2.2
Pancakes	196		0	0	0.3
Cherry pie	237		1.408	0	0.7
Chocolate cream pie	2		2.387	0	0.3
Pumpkin pie	4,515		1.608	0	1.5
Taco shell	350		3.033	0	0
Waffles	228		0	0	0.4
Wonton wrappers	14		0.082	0	0
Breakfast cereals					
All-bran	2,500		1.843	2	50
Corn flakes	2,500		0.125	0.04	50
Granola (oats, wheat germ)	37		12.875	0	95
Mixed bran (wheat, barley)	0		2.32	0	95
Oat bran	1,531		0.662	0	30.6
Oatmeal, fortified	16		0.1	3	0
Puffed rice	0		0.101	0.08	0
Puffed wheat	0		0	2	0
Raisin bran	1,364		0.912	0	0

B1 (mg)	B2 (mg)	B3 (mg)	B6 (mg)	B5 (mg)	Folic acid (µg)	B12 (µg)
0.413	0.273	4.113	0.098	0.693	26	
0.404	0.399	4.625	0.038	0.406	64	
0.243	0.145	1.04	0.21	0.676	22	
0.427	0.289	1.581	0.271	0.569	45	
0.565	0.462	5.249	0.038	0.456	31	
0.505	0.327	4.961	0.136	0.522	18	
0.388	0.241	2.188	0.058	0.861	28	
0.623	0.272	5.439	0.026	0.429	22	
0.19	0.26	2	0.044	0.27	25	
0.263	0.22	1.992	0.028	0.634	16	
0.222	0.24	1.853	0.056	0.276	8	
0.233	0.198	1.512	0.027	0.353	12	
0.14	0.12	1.1	0.022	0.335	16	
0.195	0.272	1.524	0.049	0.395	12	
0.201	0.281	1.567	0.046	0.405	12	
0.023	0.029	0.2	0.041	0.319	8	
0.036	0.107	0.678	0.02	0.393	7	
0.055	0.153	0.187	0.057	0.507	15	
0.228	0.053	1.35	0.368	0.47	6	
0.263	0.347	2.073	0.056	0.485	15	
0.519	0.378	5.424	0.03	0.025	17	
1.3	1.4	16.7	1.7	1.734	300	
1.3	1.4	16.7	1.7	0.329	353	
2.4	2.7	31.7	3.2	1.93	71	
2.4	2.7	31.7	3.2	1.93	71	
0.765	0.867	10.2	1.02	0.747	278	
0.11	0.02	0.13	0.02	0.2	4	
0.41	0.05	6.25	0	0.34	10	
2.6	1.8	35.3	0.17	0.518	32	
0.7	0.8	9.1	0.9	0.66	200	

	A (IU)	D (IU)	E (mg)	K (mg)	C (mg)
Rice cereal, crispy type	2,500		0.125	0	50
Rice cereal, extruded, check-style	60		0.13	0	53
Shredded wheat	0		0.53	0.7	0
Wheat flakes	2,500		1.231	0	50
Wheat germ, toasted	0		18.14	0	6

Vegetables

	A (IU)	D (IU)	E (mg)	K (mg)	C (mg)
Alfalfa seeds, raw	155		0.02	0	8.2
Amaranth leaves, cooked	2,770		0	800	41.1
Artichokes, cooked	177		0.19	0	10
Asparagus, cooked	539		0.38	0	10.8
Balsam-pear (bitter gourd)	1,733		0.5	0	55.6
Bamboo shoots, cooked	0		0	0	0
Beans, navy, cooked	4		0	0	17.3
Pinto beans, cooked	0		0	0	0.7
Green beans, cooked	666		0.14	38	9.7
Yellow beans, cooked	81		0.29	0	9.7
Beet greens, cooked	5,100		0.3	0	24.9
Beets, cooked	35		0.3	0	3.6
Canned beets, pickled and cooked	11		0	0	2.3
Broadbeans, cooked	270		0	0	19.8
Broccoli, cooked	1,388		1.69	205	74.6
Broccoli, raw	1,542		1.66	270	93.2
Cabbage (bok choy), cooked	2,568		0.12	0	26
Cabbage, cooked	132		0.105	0	20.1
Cabbage, raw	133		0.105	145	32.2
Red cabbage, cooked	27		0.12	0	34.4
Savoy cabbage, cooked	889		0	0	17

B1 (mg)	B2 (mg)	B3 (mg)	B6 (mg)	B5 (mg)	Folic acid (µg)	B12 (µg)
1.3	1.4	16.7	1.7	0.976	353	
1.3	0.03	17.6	1.8	0.353	353	
0.28	0.28	4.57	0.253	0.814	50	
1.25	1.42	16.67	1.67	0.796	333	
1.67	0.82	5.59	0.978	1.387	352	
0.076	0.126	0.481	0.034	0.563	36	
0.02	0.134	0.559	0.177	0.062	56.8	
0.065	0.066	1.001	0.111	0.342	51	
0.123	0.126	1.082	0.122	0.161	146	
0.147	0.282	0.995	0.76	0.06	87.6	
0.02	0.05	0.3	0.098	0.066	2.3	
0.381	0.235	1.263	0.198	0.854	106.3	
0.274	0.108	0.632	0.194	0.258	33.5	
0.074	0.097	0.614	0.056	0.074	33.3	
0.074	0.097	0.614	0.056	0.074	33.3	
0.117	0.289	0.499	0.132	0.329	14.3	
0.027	0.04	0.331	0.067	0.145	80	
0.01	0.048	0.251	0.05	0.137	26.5	
0.128	0.09	1.2	0.029	0.066	57.8	
0.055	0.113	0.574	0.143	0.508	50	
0.065	0.119	0.638	0.159	0.535	71	
0.032	0.063	0.428	0.166	0.079	40.6	
0.057	0.055	0.282	0.113	0.139	20	
0.05	0.04	0.3	0.096	0.14	43	
0.034	0.02	0.2	0.14	0.22	12.6	
0.051	0.02	0.024	0.152	0.159	46.3	

	A (IU)	D (IU)	E (mg)	K (mg)	C (mg)
Babycarrots, raw	15,010		0	0	8.4
Carrots, cooked	25,554		0.42	18	2.3
Carrots, frozen and then cooked	17,702		0.42	0	2.8
Carrots, raw	28,129		0.46	5	9.3
Cassava, raw	25		0.19	0	20.6
Catsup	1,016		1.465	0	15.1
Cauliflower, cooked	17		0.04	10	44.3
Cauliflower, raw	19		0.04	10	46.4
Celery, raw	134		0.36	12	7
Swiss chard, cooked	3,139		1.89	660	18
Chives, raw	4,353		0.21	190	58.1
Cilantro, raw	6,130		2.041	0	35.3
Collards, cooked	3,129		0.88	0	18.2
Coriander, raw	2,767		2.5	310	10.5
Sweet corn, canned	152		0	0	5.5
Sweet corn, cooked	217		0.09	0	6.2
Sweet corn, raw	281		0.09	0.5	6.8
Black eyed peas, cooked	791		0.22	0	2.2
Cucumber, raw	215		0.079	19	5.3
Dandelion greens, raw	14,000		2.5	0	35
Eggplant, cooked	64		0.03	0	1.3
Endive, raw	2,050		0.44	0	6.5
Garlic, raw	0		0.01	0	31.2
Ginger root, raw	0		0.26	0	5
Gourd calabesh, cooked	0		0	0	8.5
Hearts of palm, canned	0		0	0	7.9
Kale, cooked	7,400		0.85	650	41
Kohlrabi, cooked	35		1.67	0	54
Leeks, cooked	46		0	11	4.2
Lemon grass, raw	11		0	0	2.6
Butterhead lettuce, raw	970		0.44	122	8
Romaine lettuce, raw	2,600		0.44	0	24
Iceberg lettuce, raw	330		0.28	0	3.9

B1 (mg)	B2 (mg)	B3 (mg)	B6 (mg)	B5 (mg)	Folic acid (µg)	B12 (µg)
0.031	0.05	0.885	0.077	0.229	33	
0.034	0.056	0.506	0.246	0.304	13.9	
0.027	0.037	0.438	0.129	0.161	10.8	
0.097	0.059	0.928	0.147	0.197	14	
0.087	0.048	0.854	0.088	0.107	27	
0.089	0.073	1.367	0.175	0.143	15	
0.042	0.052	0.41	0.173	0.508	44	
0.057	0.063	0.526	0.222	0.652	57	
0.046	0.045	0.323	0.087	0.186	28	
0.034	0.086	0.36	0.085	0.163	8.6	
0.078	0.115	0.647	0.138	0.324	105	
0.063	0.182	1.306	0.132	0.57	62	
0.04	0.106	0.575	0.128	0.218	93	
0.074	0.12	0.73	0.105	0.185	10.3	
0.026	0.061	0.939	0.037	0.522	38.1	
0.215	0.072	1.614	0.06	0.878	46.4	
0.2	0.06	1.7	0.055	0.76	45.8	
0.101	0.148	1.403	0.065	0.154	127	
0.024	0.022	0.221	0.042	0.178	13	
0.19	0.26	0.806	0.251	0.084	27.2	
0.076	0.02	0.6	0.086	0.075	14.4	
0.08	0.075	0.4	0.02	0.9	142	
0.2	0.11	0.7	1.235	0.596	3.1	
0.023	0.029	0.7	0.16	0.203	11.2	
0.029	0.022	0.39	0.038	0.144	4.3	
0.011	0.057	0.437	0.022	0.126	39	
0.053	0.07	0.5	0.138	0.049	13.3	
0.04	0.02	0.39	0.154	0.16	12.1	
0.026	0.02	0.2	0.113	0.072	24.3	
0.065	0.135	1.101	0.08	0.05	75	
0.06	0.06	0.3	0.05	0.18	73.3	
0.1	0.1	0.5	0.047	0.17	135.7	
0.046	0.03	0.187	0.04	0.046	56	

	A (IU)	D (IU)	E (mg)	K (mg)	C (mg)
Looseleaf lettuce, raw	1,900		0.44	210	18
Lima beans, cooked	370		0.14	0	10.1
Lotus root, cooked	0		0.01	0	27.4
Mung beans, cooked	31		0	0	16
Oyster mushrooms, raw	48		0	0	0
Mushrooms, canned	0		0.12	0	0
Mushrooms, raw	0		0.12	0.2	3.5
Shiitake mushrooms, dried	0		0.12	0	3.5
Straw mushrooms, canned	0		0	0	0
Mustard greens, cooked	3,031		2.01	130	23.5
New Zealand spinach, cooked	3,622		0	0	16
Okra, cooked	575		0.69	0	16.3
Onions, cooked	0		0.13	2	5.2
Onions, raw	0		0.13	540	6.4
Parsley, raw	5,200		1.79	0	133
Parsnips, cooked	0		1	0	13
Peas, cooked	131		0.39	20	47.9
Peas, raw	145		0.39	25	60
Green peas, cooked	597		0.39	0	14.2
Green peas, raw	640		0.39	36	40
Banana peppers, raw	340		0.69	0	82.7
Chili peppers, canned	126		0	0	34.2
Hungarian peppers, raw	140		0	0	92.9
Jalapeno peppers, raw	215		0.473	0	44.3
Green sweet peppers, raw	632		0.69	17	89.3
Red sweet peppers, raw	5,700		0.69	0	190
Pickles	126		0.16	0	1.2
Baked potatoes	0		0.04	0	12.8
French fries, frozen and then heated in oven	0		0.19	5	10.1

B1 (mg)	B2 (mg)	B3 (mg)	B6 (mg)	B5 (mg)	Folic acid (µg)	B12 (µg)
0.05	0.8	0.4	0.055	0.2	49.8	
0.14	0.096	1.04	0.193	0.257	26.3	
0.127	0.01	0.3	0.218	0.302	7.9	
0.14	0.18	1.2	0.13	0.559	69.6	
0.055	0.36	3.579	0.122	1.291	47	
0.085	0.021	1.593	0.061	0.811	12.3	
0.102	0.449	4.116	0.097	2.2	21.1	
0.3	1.27	14.1	0.965	21.879	163.2	
0.013	0.07	0.224	0.014	0.412	38	
0.041	0.063	0.433	0.098	0.12	73.4	
0.03	0.107	0.39	0.237	0.256	8.3	
0.132	0.055	0.871	0.187	0.213	45.7	
0.042	0.023	0.165	0.129	0.113	15	
0.042	0.02	0.148	0.116	0.106	19	
0.086	0.098	1.313	0.09	0.4	152	
0.083	0.051	0.724	0.093	0.588	58.2	
0.128	0.076	0.539	0.144	0.673	29.1	
0.15	0.08	0.6	0.16	0.75	41.7	
0.259	0.149	2.021	0.216	0.153	63.3	
0.266	0.132	2.09	0.169	0.104	65	
0.081	0.054	1.242	0.357	0.265	29	
0.01	0.03	0.627	0.12	0.084	54	
0.079	0.055	1.092	0.517	0.205	53	
0.144	0.057	1.117	0.508	0.228	47	
0.066	0.03	0.509	0.248	0.08	22	
0.066	0.03	0.504	0.248	0.08	22	
0.009	0.032	0.174	0.015	0.12	1	
0.105	0.221	1.395	0.301	0.555	9.1	
0.113	0.028	2.088	0.308	0.337	12	

	A (IU)	D (IU)	E (mg)	K (mg)	C (mg)
Spinach, raw	6,715		1.89	400	28.1
Acom squash, cooked	428		0	0	10.8
Sweet potato, cooked	21,822		0.28	4	24.6
Tomato sauce, canned	997		1.4	7	13.1
Tomato, raw	623		0.38	6	19.1
Fruits					
Apricots, raw	2,612		0.89	0	10
Avocados, raw	612		1.34	40	7.9
Bananas, raw	81		0.27	0.5	9.1
Blackberries, raw	165		0.71	0	21
Blueberries, raw	100		1	6	13
Cantaloupes, raw	3,224		0.15	1	42.2
Casaba melons, raw	30		0.15	0	16
Sour cherries, raw	1,283		0.13	0	10
Sweet cherries, raw	214		0.13	0	7
Crapables, raw	40		0	0.005	8
Cranberries, raw	46		0.1	0	13.5
Cranberry sauce, canned	20		0.1	0	2
Kiwi fruit, raw	175		1.12	25	98
Mango, raw	3,894		1.12	0	27.7
Nectarine, raw	736		0.89	0	5.4
Oranges, raw	205		0.24	0.1	53.2
Peaches, raw	535		0.7	3	6.6
Pineaple, raw	23		0.1	0.1	15.4
Plums, raw	323		0.6	12	9.5
Seedless raisins, raw	8		0.7	0	3.3
Raspberries, raw	130		0.45	0	25
Rhubarb, frozen and cooked	69		0.2	0	3.3
Strawberries, raw	27		0.14	0	56.7
Tangerines, raw	920		0.24	0	30.8
Watermelon, raw	366		0.15	0	9.6
Beans and peas					
Black beans, cooked	6		0	0	0

B1 (mg)	B2 (mg)	B3 (mg)	B6 (mg)	B5 (mg)	Folic acid (µg)	B12 (µg)
0.078	0.189	0.724	0.195	0.065	194.4	
0.167	0.013	0.881	0.194	0.504	18.7	
0.073	0.127	0.604	0.241	0.646	22.6	
0.066	0.058	1.149	0.155	0.309	9.4	
0.059	0.048	0.628	0.08	0.247	15	
0.03	0.04	0.6	0.054	0.24	8.6	
0.108	0.122	1.921	0.28	0.971	61.9	
0.045	0.1	0.54	0.578	0.26	19.1	
0.03	0.04	0.4	0.058	0.24	34	
0.048	0.05	0.359	0.036	0.093	6.4	
0.036	0.021	0.574	0.115	0.128	17	
0.06	0.02	0.4	0.12	0	17	
0.03	0.04	0.4	0.044	0.143	7.5	
0.05	0.06	0.4	0.036	0.127	4.2	
0.03	0.02	0.1	0	0	0	
0.03	0.02	0.1	0.065	0.219	1.7	
0.015	0.021	0.1	0.014	0	1	
0.02	0.05	0.5	0.09	0	38	
0.058	0.057	0.584	0.134	0.16	14	
0.017	0.041	0.99	0.025	0.158	3.7	
0.087	0.04	0.282	0.06	0.25	30.3	
0.017	0.041	0.99	0.018	0.17	3.4	
0.092	0.036	0.42	0.087	0.16	10.6	
0.043	0.096	0.5	0.081	0.182	2.2	
0.156	0.088	0.818	0.249	0.045	3.3	
0.03	0.09	0.9	0.057	0.057	26	
0.018	0.023	0.2	0.02	0.02	5.3	
0.02	0.066	0.23	0.059	0.059	17.7	
0.105	0.022	0.16	0.067	0.067	20.4	
0.08	0.02	0.2	0.144	0.144	2.2	
0.244	0.059	0.505	0.069	0.242	148.8	

	A (IU)	D (IU)	E (mg)	K (mg)	C (mg)
Chickpeas, cooked	27		0.35	0	1.3
Cowpeas (blackeyes), cooked	15		0.28	0	0.4
Falafel	13		0	0	1.6
French beans, cooked	3		0	0	1.2
Great northern beans, cooked	1		0	0	1.3
Hummus, raw	25		1	0	7.9
Kidney beans, cooked	0		0.21	0	1.2
Lentils, cooked	8		0.11	0	1.5
Lima beans, cooked	0		0.18	0	0
Lupins, cooked	7		0	0	1.1
Mung beans, cooked	24		0.51	0	1
Navy beans, cooked	2		0	0	0.9
Peanut butter	0		10	0	0
Peanuts, cooked	0		3.17	0	0
Peanuts, dry-roasted	0		7.41	0	0
Peanuts, oil-roasted	0		7.41	0	0
Split peas, cooked	7		0.39	0	0.4
Pigeon peas (red gram), cooked	3		0	0	0
Pinto beans, cooked	2		0.94	0	21
Refried beans, canned	0		0	0	6
Soybeans	200		1.95	37	2.2
Soy flour, full-fat	110		0	0	0
Soy milk	32		0.1	3	0
Nuts					
Acorns, dried	0		0	0	0
Almonds, dry.roasted	0		5.55	0	0.7
Brazil nuts, dried	0		7.6	0	0.7
Butternuts, dried	124		3.5	0	3.2
Cashew nuts, dry-roasted	0		0.57	0	0
Chestnuts, roasted	24		1.2	0	26
Dried coconut meat	0		0.73	0	0

B1 (mg)	B2 (mg)	B3 (mg)	B6 (mg)	B5 (mg)	Folic acid (µg)	B12 (µg)
0.116	0.063	0.526	0.139	0.286	172	
0.202	0.055	0.495	0.1	0.411	207.9	
0.146	0.166	1.044	0.125	0.292	77.6	
0.13	0.062	0.546	0.105	0.222	74.7	
0.158	0.059	0.681	0.117	0.266	102.2	
0.092	0.053	0.411	0.398	0.288	59.4	
0.16	0.058	0.578	0.12	0.22	129.6	
0.169	0.073	1.06	0.178	0.638	180.8	
0.161	0.055	0.421	0.161	0.422	83.1	
0.134	0.053	0.495	0.009	0.188	59.3	
0.164	0.061	0.577	0.067	0.41	158.8	
0.202	0.061	0.531	0.164	0.255	139.9	
0.083	0.105	13.4	0.454	0.806	74	
0.259	0.063	5.259	0.152	0.825	74.6	
0.438	0.098	13.53	0.236	0.395	145.3	
0.253	0.108	14.28	0.255	1.39	125.7	
0.19	0.056	0.89	0.048	0.595	64.9	
0.146	0.059	0.781	0.05	0.319	110.8	
0.186	0.091	0.4	0.155	0.285	172	
0.027	0.016	0.315	0.143	0.097	11	
0.1	0.145	1.41	0.208	0.453	211	
0.412	0.941	3.286	0.351	1.209	227.4	
0.161	0.07	0.147	0.041	0.048	1.5	
0.149	0.154	2.406	0.695	0.94	114.6	
0.13	0.599	2.817	0.074	0.254	63.8	
1	0.122	1.622	0.251	0.236	4	
0.383	0.148	1.045	0.56	0.633	66.2	
0.2	0.2	1.4	0.256	1.217	69.2	
0.243	0.175	1.342	0.497	0.554	70	
0.03	0.02	0.3	0.261	0.696	7.8	

	A (IU)	D (IU)	E (mg)	K (mg)	C (mg)
Macadamina nuts, oil-roasted	9		0.41	0	0
Pecans, dry-roasted	133		3.1	0	2
Pine nuts, dried	29		0	0	2
Pistachio nuts, dry-roasted	238		5.21	70	7.3
Pumpkin and squash seeds, roasted	62		0	0	0.3
Sunflower kernels, dried	50		50.27	0	1.4
Tahini	67		2.27	0	0
Walnuts	296		2.62	0	3.2
Dairy products and eggs					
Butter	3,058	56	1.58	7	0
American cheese	1,209.6	0	0.46	0	0
Blue cheeese	721	0	0.64	0	0
Brie	667	0	0.655	0	0
Camembert	923	12	0.655	0	0
Cheddar cheese	1,059	12	0.36	3	0
Colby cheese	1,034	0	0.35	0	0
Cottage cheese 1 % fat	37	0	0.11	0	0
Cottage cheese	163	0	0.122	0	0
Cream cheese	1,427	0	0.941	0	0
Cream cheese, fat free	930	0	0.03	0	0
Edam cheese	916	36	0.751	0	0
Feta	447	0	0.03	0	0
Gouda cheese	644	0	0.35	0	0
Gruyère cheese	1,219	0	0.35	0	0
Monterey cheese	950	0	0.34	0	0
Mozzarella cheese	792	0	0.35	0	0
Muenster cheese	1,120	0	0.465	0	0
Parmasan cheese	701	28	0.8	0	0
Provolone cheese	815	0	0.35	0	0
Ricotta cheese	4.32	0	0.214	0	0
Swiss cheese	845	44	0.5	0	0

B1 (mg)	B2 (mg)	B3 (mg)	B6 (mg)	B5 (mg)	Folic acid (µg)	B12 (µg)
0.213	0.109	2.02	0.198	0.442	15.9	
0.317	0.106	0.922	0.195	1.774	40.7	
1.243	0.223	4.37	0.111	0.21	57.8	
0.423	0.246	1.408	0.255	1.212	59.1	
0.034	0.052	0.286	0.037	0.056	9	
2.29	0.25	4.5	0.77	6.745	227.4	
1.22	0.473	5.45	0.149	0.693	97.7	
0.217	0.109	0.69	0.554	0.626	65.5	
0.005	0.034	0.042	0.003	0.11	3	0.125
0.027	0.353	0.069	0.071	0.482	7.8	0.696
0.029	0.382	1.016	0.166	1.729	36.4	1.217
0.07	0.52	0.38	0.235	0.69	65	1.65
0.028	0.488	0.63	0.227	1.364	62.2	1.296
0.027	0.375	0.08	0.074	0.413	18.2	0.827
0.015	0.375	0.093	0.079	0.21	18.2	0.826
0.021	0.165	0.128	0.068	0.215	12.4	0.633
0.021	0.163	0.126	0.067	0.213	12.2	0.623
0.017	0.197	0.101	0.047	0.271	13.2	0.424
0.05	0.172	0.16	0.05	0.194	37	0.55
0.037	0.389	0.082	0.076	0.281	16.2	1.535
0.154	0.844	0.991	0.424	0.967	32	1.69
0.03	0.334	0.063	0.08	0.34	20.9	1.535
0.06	0.279	0.106	0.081	0.562	10.4	1.6
0.015	0.39	0.093	0.079	0.21	18.2	0.826
0.015	0.243	0.084	0.056	0.064	7	0.654
0.013	0.32	0.103	0.056	0.19	12.1	1.473
0.045	0.386	0.315	0.105	0.527	8	1.4
0.019	0.321	0.156	0.073	0.476	10.4	1.463
0.021	0.185	0.078	0.02	0.242	13.1	0.291
0.022	0.365	0.092	0.083	0.429	6.4	1.676

	A (IU)	D (IU)	E (mg)	K (mg)	C (mg)
Sour cream cheese	790	0	0.566	1	0.86
Whole fried eggs	857	32	1.64	0	0
Hard-boiled whole eggs	560	0	1.05	0	0
Whole eggs, raw	635	52	1.05	2	0
Egg yolk, raw	1,945	0	1.05	0	0
Skim milk w/ Vit A	204	40	0.04	0.02	0.98
Whole milk, 3.3 % fat	126	40	0.1	0.3	0.94
Yogurt	123	0	0.088	0	0.53
Buttermilk from skim milk	33	0	0.06	0	0.98
Goat milk	185	0	0.18	0	1.88
Fish and seafood					
Oyster, breaded and fried	302	0	0	0	3.8
Perch, cooked	32	0	0	0	1.7
Northern pike, cooked	81	0	0	0	3.8
Walleye pollock, cooked	76	0	0.2	0	0
Roe, raw	263	0	7	0	16
Chinook salmon, smoked	88	0	1.35	0	0
Rainbow smelt, cooked	58	0	0	0	0
Snapper, cooked	115	0	0	0	1.6
Squid, fried	35	0	0	0	4.2
Surimi	66	0	0	0	0
Swordfish, cooked	137	0	0	0	1.1
Rainbow trout, cooked	50	0	0	0	2
Tuna, cooked	2,520	0	0	0	0
Whiting, cooked	114	0	0	0	0
Sardine, canned in oil	224	272	0.3	0	0
Scallop, breaded and fried	75	0	0	0	2.3
Sea bass, cooked	213	0	0	0	0
Shark, battered and fried	180	0	0	0	0
Shrimp, breaded and fried	189	0	0	0	1.5
Shrimp, cooked	219	152	0.51	0	2.2

B1 (mg)	B2 (mg)	B3 (mg)	B6 (mg)	B5 (mg)	Folic acid (µg)	B12 (µg)
0.035	0.149	0.067	0.016	0.36	10.8	0.3
0.057	0.523	0.077	0.143	1.224	38	0.92
0.066	0.513	0.064	0.121	1.398	44	1.11
0.062	0.508	0.073	0.139	1.255	47	1
0.17	0.639	0.015	0.392	1.807	146	3.11
0.036	0.14	0.088	0.04	0.329	5.2	0.378
0.038	0.162	0.084	0.042	0.314	5	0.357
0.029	0.142	0.075	0.032	0.389	7,4	0.372
0.034	0.154	0.058	0.034	0.275	5	0.219
0.047	0.316	0.194	0.05	0.638	7.9	0.163
0.15	0.202	1.65	0.064	0.27	13.6	15.629
0.08	0.12	1.9	0.14	0.87	5.8	2.2
0.067	0.077	2.8	0.135	0.87	17.3	2.3
0.074	0.076	1.65	0.069	0.16	3.6	4.2
0.24	0.74	1.8	0.16	1	80	10
0.023	0.101	4.72	0.278	0.87	1.9	3.26
0.01	0.146	1.766	0.17	0.74	4.6	3.969
0.053	0.004	0.346	0.46	0.87	5.8	3.5
0.056	0.458	2.602	0.058	0.51	5.3	1.228
0.02	0.021	0.22	0.03	0.07	1.6	1.6
0.043	0.116	11.79	0.381	0.38	2.3	2.019
0.152	0.097	5.77	0.346	1.065	19	6.3
0.278	0.306	10.54	0.525	1.37	2.2	10.878
0.068	0.074	1.67	0.18	0.25	15	2.6
0.08	0.227	5.245	0.167	0.642	11.8	8.94
0.042	0.11	1.505	0.14	0.2	18.2	1.318
0.13	0.15	1.9	0.46	0.87	5.8	0.3
0.072	0.097	2.783	0.3	0.62	5.2	1.211
0.129	0.136	3.07	0.098	0.35	8.1	1.87
0.031	0.032	2.59	0.127	0.34	3.5	1.488

Minerals

Beside of carbohydrates, fat, water, protein, phytochemical and vitamins, do the body needs minerals to function. Minerals play a great part in the act of making the body function and prosper, and 21 minerals are considered essential to the body. This meaning that the body can't grow, reproduce itself and sustain it's own life if they aren't provided in the diet. Plant based diets can of course provide all these minerals. And if they couldn't, how would the animals that omnivores consumes that eats a plant based diet themselves, obtain them and store them in their body?

Iron
Adults need **1.8 milligrams iron daily**.

Vegan dietary sources of iron is beans, leafy green vegetables, potatoes, squash, tofu, lentils, soybeans, brown rice, whole grain flour, wheat germ etc. Vegetarian sources of iron are dairy and eggs, and pescetarian sources of iron is fish.
Iron plays a great part as a vital component of blood cells, carriing ocygen around the body and carbon dioxide away from the body. Besides of this, iron is a component in the immune system, in enzymes and cells of the body. The body looses iron when cells like skincells dies and falls of the body, and girls and womens in the child-bearing age loose iron when they bleed during the menstrual cykle. Vegan diets often contains more iron than diets based on meat, dairy and eggs making vegans less likely to suffer from iron shortage.

Calcium
Adults need about **1000 milligrams calcium daily**, and individuals older than 50 years should consume 1,200 milligrams of calcium daily. Vegan sources of calcium are leafy green vegetables, beans, potatoes, soy products, oranges etc. Vegetarian sources of calcium are dairy, but as

you are able to read in "the perils of dairy" chaptor, dairy is a exceptionally poor source of calcium, even though dairy products normally are high in calcium.

Calcium makes up large parts of the bones and teeth of the body. A small percentage, 1 percent of the calcium in the body are found other places than the bones and teeth and serve vital functions there, serving in the nerve system, as a part of cell metabolism and plays a part in the process of blood clotting when the body needs to stop a bleeding. Reaching maximum bone strength takes about 20 to 30 years. 45 percent of the bone mass are gained until age 11 years, and another 45 percent are gained until age 16 years. After age 16, an additional 10 percent are gained until age 30 years. After age 30, the bones of the body gradually begins to lose strength, and if a bad diet like the Western diet high in animal protein are consumed, bones will soon end up in a bad condition.

Chromium
Adults need **35 micrograms chromium** daily.

Vegan sources of chromium is grains, mushrooms, prunes, spices, yeast, beer, prunes etc.
Chromium is needed to support the function of insulin.

Zinc
Adults need **11 milligrams of zinc** daily.

Vegan dietary sources of zinc is beans, potatoes, squash, tofu, lentils, brown rice, soybeans, whole grain flour, wheat germ, leafy green vegetables etc. Vegetarian sources of iron are dairy and eggs. Vegetarian dietary sources of zinc is eggs and dairy products.
Zinc is involved in many vital reactions in the body. It is a component of perhaps several hundreds enzyme systems, essential to cell division and many other things. Zinc is essential for respiration, healing of wounds,

the immune system, synthesis of blood, synthesis of protein and helps to build the DNA of the body.

Copper
Adults need **0.9 milligrams of copper** daily.

Vegan dietary sources of grains, nuts, tofu, tempeh, beans, bananas, raisins, sweet potatoes and prunes. Vegetarian sources are eggs and dairy. Pescetarian sources are fish.
Copper is needed in protein metabolism, in order for the body to make use of iron and is a key component in many hormones. Vegan, vegetarian and pescetarian diets are often plentiful in copper.

Iodine
Adults should consume **150 micrograms iodine** daily. The safe uppper limit of iodine consumption is 1,100 micrograms.

Vegan dietary sources of iodine is iodized salt and seaweed. Vegetarian sources of iodine are eggs and dairy products. Pescetarian sources of iodine are fish and other animals of the sea.
Iodine is very important during pregnancy and lactating. Iodine is a key component of thyroid hormones that is controlling many organ systems.

Magnesium
Adults should consume **400 to 420 milligrams of magnesium** daily.

Vegan sources of magnesium is whole grains, nuts, leafy green vegetables, vegetables, legumes, seeds, fruit and chocolate. Vegetarian sources are dairy and eggs. Pescetarian sources are fish and shellfish. Magnesium helps keep the bones and teeth strong, are a part of the nerve system and plays a role in the process of converting food to energy.

Selenium
Adults should consume **55 micrograms selenium** daily. The upper safe level of daily selenium consumption is 400 micrograms daily.

Vegan sources of selenium are whole grains and nuts. Vegetarian sources are eggs and dairy, and pescetarian sources are fish.
Selenium is an antioxidant and do therefore protects the cells of the body from oxidate damage.

Sodium
Adults should consume **500 milligrams sodium** daily. No more than 2,400 milligrams of sodium should be consumed.

Vegan sources of sodium are salt, canned tomatoes, tomato sauce, highly processed foods like veggie burgers and soy sauce. Vegetarian sources of sodium are eggs and dairy products. Pescetarian sources of sodium are fish and other animals of the sea.
Sodium is needed by the nerve system, the digestion system and is used by the body to maintain the fluid balance outside of the cells.

Potassium
Adults should consume **at least 2,000 milligrams potassium** daily.

Vegan sources of potassium are mushrooms, tomatoes, strawberries, bean, potatoes and bananas. Vegetarian dietary sources of potassium is eggs and dairy products. Potassium is also found in fish.
Potassium is used by the body to contract the muscles, to maintain fluid balance inside the cells and is used in the nerve system.

Growing up on plants

Most people experience that individuals in their network have particular concerns about being vegan, vegetarian or even pescetarian and having a baby. Your family, friends and the healthcare professionals that are helping you might never had experienced a pregnant women eating plant based, and might be even more worried than at the time you had to convince them that you could survive and prosper without consuming milk. Some mothers and fathers to be might even start doubting themselves, but there is off course no need at all to be worried if you just have access to the information you need. And you will need not to doubt yourself, cause just as an animal product based Western diet is not healthy for grown ups, it sure is not healthy for babies or children. And babies need food meant for human beings, and not something which according to the statistic could be extremely likely to cause them health problems throughout their life and make an end to them. Major studies of vegan babies have showed that a vegan diet does not need to affect birth weight, and that potential side effects of pregnancy like preeclampsia was almost entirely absent in vegan mothers. The studies did also conclude that it is possibly to maintain a normal pregnancy on a vegan diet, and that a vegan diet removes most are all signs of preeclampsia. Other studies have showed that vegan mothers consuming too few calories can give birth to children that are smaller than average, which leads to conclude that vegan mothers like all other human beings shall attend to what they eat, and remember to eat a diet that suits their need.

Pregnant and lactating
Babies who have not yet been born live and grow exclusively on the diet their mother consumes. The eating patterns of their mothers will most likely be adopted by the baby when it grows older and bigger, which makes it critical to eat right so yourself, your child and the rest of your family adopts eating patterns that are healthy. It is a good idea to

change your normal vegan diet to a vegan diet tailored for pregnancy when you start to think about getting pregnant maybe one or two years in advance of the conception, so that you body builds up the nutritional reserves needed to carry out a successful pregnancy. This will make you body be in proper shape when you do get pregnant, and you will already have completed the transition into eating a vegan diet tailored for pregnancy. You new diet will need to be about 10 to 15 percent higher in calorie intake, and contain as much as the double amount of some vitamins and minerals.

Pregnant women need to gain weight throughout their pregnancy. This is crucial to the health of the baby, and women who fail to gain weight during their pregnancy is likely to have a baby with too low birth weight. And babies with too low birth weight, like babies born weighing less than 2.5 kilo are more likely to suffer from illness or die an early death. Weight gain happens as always by consuming more calories than you use. During the first trimester, you should consume about 100 extra calories per day, and during the next two trimesters you should consume about 300 calories extra than you normally do. If you are having trouble gaining weigh or are bad at eating large amounts of food, then try to eat foods that are higher in calories per weight unit. Seeds, butters, nuts, oils, avocados, bananas and dishes with high fat ingredients should help make the trick easier.

Just as most people have the idea that humans needs extreme amounts of protein, do many individuals also think that pregnant women have need for extreme amounts of protein. Pregnant women should consume about 60 to 66 grams of protein daily, which only is a moderate increase from what nonpregnant women needs to consume. One extra serving of protein rich food like lentils, beans, tofu should add the extra grams of protein needed in order to satisfy both the protein needs of the growing baby and the mother growing the baby.

Minerals

Pregnant and lactating women need to consume more iron than a non-pregnant woman. During pregnancy, the body becomes more effective to absorb the iron consumed thru the diet, and the body looses less iron because the menstrual cycle stops. But the development of the new life do still increase the need for iron, and the recommended daily intake of iron increases from 32 milligrams daily to 49 milligrams daily. Good dietary sources of iron are legumes, tofu, seeds, nuts, whole grains, dark green leafy vegetables and dried fruit.

Zinc, can also be an issue in both pregnant and lactating vegans and pregnant omnivores. The recommended intake of zinc daily during pregnancy is 11 milligrams daily, which accounts for an increase of three milligrams daily. Whole sources of food such as whole grains, nuts, seeds and legumes are good dietary sources of zinc.

Calcium serves the same functions in the growing baby as it does in the mother. It is needed to build bones, theths and nerve, blood and muscle functioning. Great calcium reserves are stored in the mothers bones and teeth, so there should not be any chance of the baby needing any calcium. But in order to protect your own bones from being eaten up, it is essential to eat calcium rich foods in greater amounts than you normally should do, and you should aim at eating at least six servings of calcium rich foods. If you are having trouble getting enough calcium from the diet, you could take supplements providing about 500 to 600 milligrams of calcium in addition to the calcium you get in the food.

Pregnant and lactating women should aim at a daily intake of 5 micrograms (200 IU) of Vitamin D daily, just as nonpregnant women should do. Pregnant women living in spending most time indoor or who lives in cold parts of the world and receives little sunshine expulsion should get about 10 micrograms (400 IU) of Vitamin D daily. Vitamin D is needed for the calcium to be absorbed by the body, and is as well as any other vitamins vital for the body. It might generally be a good idea to take a supplement of Vitamin D, if you are having trouble getting enough Vitamin D from either the sun, mushrooms or fortified foods.

Vitamin B12 during pregnancy and lactating should come from either fortified foods or vitamin supplements. There is no known viable plant source of Vitamin B12, and the unborn child is depending on getting Vitamin B12 from its mother. Pregnant women should consume at least three micrograms Vitamin B12 from supplements of fortified foods daily. Pregnant women's consuming too little Vitamin B12 is likely to have a baby with Vitamin B12 stores only 10 to 25 percents of what a baby of woman consuming enough B12 would have. The Vitamin B12 stored in a newborn baby from a mother consuming too little Vitamin B12 will only last for a very limited period of time, while the Vitamin B12 stores found in babies born to women consuming enough B12 would last from six months to one whole year. Vitamin B12 deficiency in babies is even more dangerous than Vitamin B12 deficiency in adults, and it cannot be stated often enough that there at the time is no known valid vegetable sources of Vitamin B12, whereas needs must be met by consumption of fortified foods, supplements or by an injection by a doctor. Vitamin B12 deficiency will most of the time cause loss of reflexes, weakness, muscle wasting, brain damage, delayed development and a general failure to thrive.

Supplements of Vitamin B9 are normally recommended for all pregnant and lactating women so they end up consuming about 600 micrograms. But vegan and vegetarian tends to consume much more Vitamin B9 than do omnivores, so vegan and vegetarian pregnant women might not need to consume as much Vitamin B9 from supplements as do omnivorous women's. Studies have showed that vegans consumed an average of 435 micrograms of Vitamin B9 daily and that omnivores only consumed an average of 240 micrograms of Vitamin B9 daily. Vegan and vegetarian pregnant women could either choose to increase their dietary intake of Vitamin B9 when they planning on getting pregnant and when they are pregnant, or they could choose to take supplements of Vitamin B9 instead. Good dietary sources of Vitamin B9 are legumes and leafy green vegetables.

Supplements of vitamins and minerals are not needed if you know how to plan your diet, eat properly and live in a country where fortified foods is available. But generally it is a good idea to take a multivitamin just to be sure that everything is okay, or maybe even more than okay. But people who are not healthy at the time of the conception and throughout the pregnancy should take vitamin and mineral supplements. This accounts for people who are underweight and undernourished, people with a history of low iron, individuals with a nutritional deficiency of any kind, smokers, heavy drinkers, individuals unable to consume enough food to meet their needs, individuals with limited exposure to sunlight and individuals unable to consume food fortified with Vitamin B12.

Nothing beats breast milk
All babies should be breast-fed for a minimum of one year and it is highly recommendable to continue breastfeeding for two years or more. Just like cow milk is designed to meet the special needs of cows, human breast milk is specially designed to meet the special needs of humans. It helps avoid or increases the chance of avoiding a number of allergies and avoiding gastrointestinal and respiratory diseases. Those benefits continues until natural weaning occurs when the baby is between two to four years of age. If you for some reason should choose to stop breastfeeding before time, should end up being unable to breastfeed or for some reason choose to cut down on breastfeeding to fewer than three times a day you must use a commercial formula to replace the breast feeding. A such replacement does in no way match the extreme benefit breast milk provides to a child, but it is better than nothing. The formula should of course contain both Vitamin B12 and

Vitamin D, and if it does not contain this supplements should be given. Breast fed babies should receive supplements of about 0.3 micrograms of Vitamin B12 daily from their second week of life until at least two years of age or until, if you live in a country were it is available, they eat enough Vitamin B12 from fortified foods to meet their needs. New-born babies have unlike adults, quite low stores of Vitamin B12 which means that they soon will run out if they aren't given enough Vitamin B12, possibly causing irreversible damage. The breast milk does provide Vitamin B12, but if the mothers diet is low in Vitamin B12, so is the breast milk likely to be. It would also be a good idea to give Vitamin D supplements of about 5 micrograms daily in warm climates and 10 micrograms daily in northern climates. This should be given from the beginning of the baby's second week of life, and continued until needs are met by fortified foods if it is available, or by exposure to the sun. It should be clearly stated that the only acceptable alternative to human breast milk is commercial infant formula, and that this should only be used if there is no way the baby can have breast milk. You should newer try to make you're own formula, because it is very, very likely to go wrong and cause great harm to you're baby. Most of the cases used to scare vegan and vegetarian mothers away from raising vegan and vegetarian children, is babies raised on homemade formula that did not meet the need of the child, and ended up causing a lot more harm than good.

Solid food and weaning
When you begin to feel that your baby can handle solid food, which it will be able to at about four to six moths of age depending on how quickly they are growing and a number of other factors. Solid foods provide extra energy, protein, minerals and other nutrients which is needed by the baby in order to grow, and beside of this is it important for a baby to experience the new food. Signs of the baby being ready to experience new and solid foods beside of breast milk is when it is able to sit up and express that it is fed up, by turning its head. Or when it is

hungry all of the time, even after have been nursed after eight to ten times daily. And when it is able to move solids around in its mouth and swallow it without spitting most of the food out again.

Vegetables, cereals, fruits and other traditional baby foods are great sources of solid foods for a baby. When solid foods are introduced, you should remember to keep an eye on allergies. Some babies might be allergic to nuts or other things, and therefore feeding them to the baby would cause them harm. When a new food is introduced, wait about a week before introducing a new food. This will give you time to notice any allergic reactions, and to decide whether the particular product should be left out of the diet. If there is a strong family history of food allergies for a particular product, it is highly recommendable to wait until the child is two to three years before introducing it. All foods that are associated with choking babies such as whole grapes, nuts, seeds, popcorns, whole pieces of meat replacement, hard candies etc. should be avoided before 12 months of age. Juice consumption should be limited because it easily takes up space for more nutritious products, and foods with added sugar, salt and hydrogenated fats should be avoided. It is highly recommendable to introduce the baby to food with some texture before it becomes nine months. At this age the baby will develop preferences for the different texture found in more "normal" food, and therefore is it important to present this kind of foods to the baby.

At the time where the baby's consumption of breast milk decreases, and after weaning is it important to feed the baby a diet high enough in calories. The main problem that have been seen in vegan and vegetarian babies beside of vitamin and mineral deficiency, is a lag of calories. Breast milk contains a lot of calories, and over 50 percent of the calories found in breast milk per unit is from fat, and a cup of breast milk contains about 175 calories a cup. After weaning, the baby will still need a lot of calories. Appropriate foods with high amounts of energy are breast milk, formula, avocado, tofu, butters, creams, soups and food with canola and flax oil. Unlike adults, food served for babies should not be too high in fibre. This is because the baby is poor at digesting it, whereas it mainly serves to fill up the very limited space in the baby's stomach. And when food rich in fiber is served for the baby, do always use whole grain because the important minerals and vitamins is mainly found in this version, and not in highly processed grains like white flour. Babies have very small stomachs and should therefore be fed about five or six times daily.

The perils of dairy products

The nutritional advisors that are practising today once went to college and university. They would, if the received nutritional education from established public institutions, often learns things like "Milk is the most nutritious food in the diet at any age[1]," and "Most authorities agree that milk is the single most important food in the diet[1]". The quotes are taken from a standard college textbook, and it is quotes like this that makes doctors and dieticians recommend wrong and dangerous things to the people they are supposed to help. Milk is like other animal products highly associated with the Western lifestyle diseases, but only few healthcare professionals question if dairy products truly are so healthy as they marketed as. They seem to ignore that large parts of the world, like Asia, South America and Africa live a healthy life's without milk and that milk were not that common in the diets of Americans and Europeans only a few hundred years ago.

Little dairy was used in 17th centery Europe
For an example did only four of 100 recipes found in a western cookbook published in 1616 contains milk. Cream is used in one of the recipes and butter is used in 25 of the recipes[2]. If you count the number of recipes that include the use of milk in a modern day cookbook, you will find that a find a significantly higher amount of milk and other dairy products is being used. Out of a total of 860 recipes found in a modern day cookbook, as many as 554 includes the use of milk and other kinds of dairy products[3]. When you look at historical reports from start 19th century Northern Europe, you will find that milk and dairy products only plays a small part in the kitchen. Only the rich consumed dairy products, and all of the milk produced by the society was made into butter and cheese. The cows of that age were at summertime fed a diet of grass, and when the winter came, they were fed a diet of straw. The farmers could only save enough straw to keep their cows alive during the winter, which resulted in a very low amount of milk being

produced during the winter. In addition to this, did the milk went bad after only a few days because of lag of any effective cooling[4].

Cows have over time been breed to produce larger amounts of milk. Statistic concerning the production of milk in Denmark, Scandinavia, Northern Europe in the 1850-ties tells that the dairy cows at that time produced 1,000 kilo milk annually. The numbers concern a big well-run herd, and it is very likely that small farms with only one or two cows produced lower amounts of milk[5]. Today, cows produce about 8,900 kilos of milk annually, or about nine times as much as they did in 1850[6]. This large production of milk per cow also accounts for the relatively low increase in the number of cows, seen in contrast to the relatively high increase in milk consumption. The amount of dairy cows in the US became halved from year 1959 to year 1990, a period of time where the American production of milk and dairy products doubled[7]. The dairy farmers wanted, naturally, to breed cows that produced the greatest amount of milk and made the greatest profit. This led to a systematically breeding programme, and the cow that had already been bred from the Aurochs ended up being bred into the kinds of dairy cattle used today.

Dairy cows used today have larger udders than the cows used hundred of years ago. A larger udder can produce and store larger amounts of milk, but the large production of milk wears the cow down. Today, dairy cattle are taken out of milk production and slaughtered after only one or two years serving as a dairy cow. Normally, dairy cattle are able to produce milk a minimum of 10 to 12 years. To deliver this enormous amount of milk, the diet of the dairy cattle have also been changed, and now do only few cows eat grass. Instead, dairy cattle are fed a diet of corn and soy that do have a negative influence of the healthiness of the milk.

Omega fatty acids in dairy
The change in the diet of the cows has changed the ratio between the fatty acids found in milk and dairy products. And even though many people consume low-fat or skim milk, the changed ratio between the fatty acids plays a great part when it comes to cheese and other dairy products with high levels of fat. The ratio between omega-3 and omega-6 fatty acids has changed as a result of a soy and corn diet fed to the dairy cows today. Today, much more omega-6 than omega-3 is found in dairy products, and omega-6 is sadly the lesser healthy one. Omega-3 is essential for the development of nerve cells and serves as an inhibiter of inflammation and cell growth[8]. Omega-6 serves among other things as promoter of cancer cell growth, growth of the fatty tissue of the body and inflammation[9, 10]. Some hundred years ago, when the cows lives on a diet of grass and straws equally amounts or the two fatty acids were found in the dairy products. But today, the amount of omega-6 in for example butter is seven times higher than the amount of omega-3 in butter[11]. On average, the Western diet typically have an omega-6 to omega-3 ratio of 10 to 1, and some as high as 30 to 1. Researchers believe that the optimal ratio is four to one or lover[12, 13].

Dairy does not help individuals keep weight at a healthy level, and is a contributing factor in lifestyle diseases like cancer
An American study conducted from 1976 to 1991 showed the effect omega-6' have on fat cell growth. The participants intake of fat decreased with 11 percent and their intake of calories fell with four percent, but the participants became 31 percent fatter over the course of the study[14]. In addition to this, do the artificial growth hormone, rBST used in the US also plays a prominent part in making individuals consuming dairy products obese and overweight[15]. Casein found in milk acts as a cancer promoter thru the growth hormone IGF-1[16]. When carcinogenic substances found in the environment causes cancer in the cells of the body, IGF-1 helps the cancer to grow and spread to a larger area of the body. About 70 years ago, growth hormones like IGF-1 did

only constitute a small danger because only few carcinogenic substances were found in the environment. But the technological progress and years of pollution have changed this, why a vide variety of carcinogenic substances today is able to give IGF-1 cancer cells to promote.

Dairy cows have to get pregnant once in a while to maintain the population of milk-giving dairy cows. When the cow approaches the day where it is due to give birth, the amount of oestrogen in its blood and its milk rise dramatically[17]. Earlier, this did not constitute a problem because cows were not milked in the last months of their pregnancy, and therefore, no milk where being sold containing radical amounts of oestrogen. But today, cows are often milked up until the very day it gives birth, which results in far greater amounts of oestrogen in today's milk than the milk produced earlier.

Dairy and Vitamin D

When asked why they drink milk, most people answer because it is healthy and is needed to build strong bones. But the fact is that milk and other dairy products are terrible sources of calcium needed for building strong bones. The mineral part of the bones is a chemical compound build by unification between calcium and phosphate, known as hydroxylapatite[18, 19]. The calcium found in milk needs to be assimilated in the blood before it can end up in the bones, and if the calcium is not assimilated in the blood it will end up in the stool. About 99 percent of the calcium found in the body is stored in the bones and the teeth's, and the remaining one percent is really important. This one percent helps the nerve system, is used in various enzymes and to maintain the function of the cells. If the concentration of calcium in the blood is too low, the body either takes calcium from the diet, and if this is not enough, take calcium from the bones of the body. And if the concentration of calcium in the blood is too high, more calcium will be added to the bones, if the bones can use anymore calcium and if the right conditions are present. The hormone PHT, Parathyroid hormone, control these processes. If the amount of calcium in the blood is too low, the amount of PHT increases, and if the amount of calcium in the blood is too high, the amount of PHT decreases[20].

Vitamin D is produced in the skin when the sun shines on it, and it is stored in the liver as 25-D until the body needs it. The PHT do when in need of Vitamin D, start a process where it is transformed into an active form called 1,25-D, which takes place in the kidneys. This chemical compound decides how much calcium is absorbed into the blood from the gut, because the compound makes the cell membrane permeable for minerals like calcium. Inadequate amount of Vitamin D is dangerous, because the vitamin plays an important part in both the immune system, brain cells and other cells. Researchers have found an association between insufficient amounts of Vitamin D and the Western lifestyle diseases. Diseases like prostate cancer, breast cancer, ovarian cancer, colorectal cancer and esophageal cancer are much more common in countries with only few hours of sunshine daily. Sclerosis rheumatism and colitis is also associated with inadequate amounts of Vitamin D, and a Finnish study showed that children with sufficient amounts of vitamin D had 80 percent lover risk of diabetes, and children with rickets, a disease largely caused by a lag of Vitamin D have four times greater risk of having diabetes[21]. In addition, the areas of the world where people on average have a small intake of Vitamin D, have a much larger prevalence of hypertension[22]. Studies have also shown that light therapy can help people with hypertension, doubling the amount of 1,25-D in their blood[23].

Lag of Vitamin D in the Western world is common in all ages. The Western diet which is causing the many lifestyle diseases does not contain large amounts of Vitamin D, and most westerners spend most of their time indoor away from the sun. In addition to this, individuals who do get enough Vitamin D from dietary sources and the sun, is still likely to have insufficient amounts of 1,25-D in the blood if they consume the Western diet. The PHT controls the amount of 1,25-D in the blood, and a large and concentrated intake of calcium as found in dairy products will result in low amounts of PHT in the blood. The dairy products make do this way cause a low concentration of PHT in the blood, which results in low amounts of 1,25-D in the blood, which the body needs in high amounts to use for vital process in the brain and in the cells. Something that would not happen on a vegan diet, because a vegan diet does not contain highly concentrated amounts of calcium that hurts the body.

70 percent of the world would be in great pain if they ate dairy

Overall, most mammals do produce lactase, the enzyme used to digest lactose, only as long as they drink milk from their mother. When they stop drinking milk from their mother, they stop producing lactase and simply lose the ability to digest milk. This is why no other adult animal than the human can digest milk, and most evidence points towards the fact, that all humans originally had it this way. Today, 70 percent of the adult human population of the earth is unable to digest milk. The percentage of people unable to digest milk is highest among Asians, where 95 percent of the adult population is unable to digests milk. About 60 to 80 percent of individuals living on the African continent are unable to digest milk, and 60 to 70 percent of the population of the countries living in South India is unable to digest milk. Among these people, the ability to produce lactase and digest milk lapse when they turn three, and only people born to families who have lived in Northern Europe and Northern America for many generations maintain the ability to produce lactase throughout their entire life. In North America, about 6 to 22 percent of the adult white population is lactose intolerant, and in Northern Europe, 2 to 15 percent of the adult white population lactose intolerant[24].

Osteoporosis is one of the lifestyle diseases that occur in the wake of the self-destructive eating patterns of the Western world. Osteoporosis affects the life of a great percentage of the American population. Estimates suggest that almost 10 million Americans have osteoporosis, and that 1.5 million individuals are hit by an ostereorotic fracture each year in the US[25, 26, 27]. Among 50 years old white American women, the lifetime risk of osteoporotic diseases such as hip, forearm or spine fracture is 40 percent[28]. Hip fracture is the most serious of these osteoporotic diseases because they most of the time results in hospitalization and death for 20 percent of the cases and to permanent disability for 50 percent of the affected[29]. Osteoporosis, means that the bones gradually loses their strength due to loss of bone mineral among other things. Individuals suffering from osteoporosis have increased risk of bone fracture, and the bone fractures takes longer to heal. Individuals who have gotten osteoporosis mostly first discover they have the disease, when the bones of the body begin to break and it therefore is too late. The US, Denmark, Sweden, New Zealand have the most cases of osteoporosis and kidney stones in spite of large dietary intake of calcium from dairy products in these countries[30, 31]. The countries with the fewest cases of osteoporosis and kidney stones are the countries located in those areas of the world where the population traditionally does not consume any dairy products[30, 31].

Dairy helps the bones to break apart

Even though osteoporosis is caused by several factors, do the consumption of food high in acid like animal protein play a significant part[36, 32, 33]. The high intake of acid needs to be neutralized with among other things calcium from the bones, which leads to the loss of bone mineral[34]. High dietary intake of acid also increases the level of the steroid cortisol in the body, and Individuals with a high intake of antioxidants such as lycopene and carotenoids, found in plants, have a lower risk of hip fracture and osteoporosis. A team of researchers studied data from 370 men and 576 gathered with a mean age of 75 years over the course of 17 years. A total of 100 hip fractures occurred during the 17 years the study ran, and those with the highest intake of carotenoids had the lowest risk of hip fracture, and individuals with higher intake of lycopene had a lower risk of hip fracture and nonvertebral fracture[35].

Two cells handle the building and decomposition of the bones, osteoblast and osteoclast. Osteoblast is the name of the cell that handles the building of the bones. It is activated when the concentration of calcium in the blood is higher than what the body needs, where it use this excess amount of calcium to build the bones[36]. The other cell, osteoclast removes calcium from the bones creating small holes in the bones, when there are inadequate amounts of calcium in the blood, and not enough calcium can be obtained from the diet. It creates small dints in the bones[37]. Both cells are controlled by PHT, but the activity of osteoclast is also affected by acid. Studies have shown that osteoclast is inactive when the environment surrounding it is slightly alkaline, like at pH 7.3, and most active in a slightly acidic environment, like at pH 6.9. This relatively small difference in pH does a great deal of difference, because at pH 7.1, the normal pH of the bones, a change in pH as small as 0.05 can result in a doubling of the dints that osteoclast makes. The process that makes the blood acidic is called acidosis, and acidosis can be caused by a high intake of protein, and especially by a high intake of animal protein[38].

Both animal protein and vegetable protein contains sulfur[39]. Some of this sulfur is absorbed into the blood as sulphuric acid, where it makes the pH of the blood rise and causes the blood become more acidic. Foods like cheese, meat, eggs and milk especially makes the blood more acidic, and foods such as vegetables and fruits help to lover the pH of the blood, neutralizing some of the acid in the blood[40]. A study of women older than 50 years hit by a hip fracture and what they ate, found exactly what the theoretical science suggests. Women from 33 different countries participated in the study, and the team of researchers conducting the study found that when the amount of animal protein in the diet reached above 30 percent, the amount of hip fractures rose dramatically. Again, is it the Western diet high in animal protein that causes the lifestyle diseases affecting the Western diet. Germany is found as a top scorer with almost 200 hip fractures per 100,000 capita. Norway comes in second with 186 hip fractures per 100,000 capita and Denmark lies third with 165 hip fractures per 100,000 capita[41]. In another study, 15 young and apparently healthy individuals were divided into three groups and asked to eat diets with different amounts of animal protein. The researchers conducting that the study found that the group eating the lowest amount of animal protein, the group placed on a vegetarian diet, secreted 103 mg. of calcium daily, and that the group eating meat and other animal products secreted 150 mg calcium daily. The study also found that the group eating meat and animal products had lost bone mineral over the course of the study[42]. Kidney stones are also an issue when it comes to calcium loss, and studies shows that more than 90 percent of the kidney stones found in individuals consuming the Western diet, is due to their high intake of protein, and the calcium the animal protein removes from the bones[43]. Other studies have shown that a high fruit and vegetable intake has positive effects on bone health[44, 45, 46, 47, 48, 49, 50, 51, 52].

Humans are meant to drink milk from their mothers

The composition of nutrients in the milk of different mammals is different because the children of different species have different needs. The young whale needs other nutrients than the young mouse or the young human. The faster an animal needs to grow, the more protein do it need in its milk. The young mink doubles its weight in only two days, why the milk it drinks contains 19.1 percent protein. The young cow doubles its weight in 47 days, why the milk it drinks contains 3.5 percent protein. The young human doubles its weight in 180 days, why the milk it drinks from its mother only contains 1.6 percent protein[53]. The human breast milk have a different composition than the milk of other animals, because the young human has other needs than the young calf or the young whale. The composition of the protein found in human breast milk is also different from the composition of milk from the cow. Cow milk contains great amounts of casein which infant gets sick from eating, and therefore only is found in small amounts in human breast milk. Another substance found in cow milk is Beta-lactoglobulin which acts as an allergy promoter just as casein[54, 55].

15 to 40 percent of the children of the Western world show symptoms of hypersensitivity of milk[56, 57]. But only five percent of those kids are found to be allergic of milk when tested with mainstream allergy tests, which leaves 10 to 35 percent that do not react on classic allergic tests, but who still shows signs of allergies, and which most doctors will not diagnose as allergic, because the mainstream allergic test do not react on the dairy products, which might be causing the allergic reactions. A French physician, Nicolas Le Berre have collected a great collection of stories from his career, where he has treated various diseases by removing dairy products, avoiding sugar and recommending that patients replaced white flour with whole grain flour. By sticking to these simple rules, the patients of Nicolas have treated their diseases such as acne, menstrual pains, cysts in the breasts and the ovary, sinusitis and allergies among other things[58].

Infants who have newer had cows milk or infant formula based on cows milk can still develop allergies of cows milk. All it takes, is that the mother of the young child has consumed dairy products while being pregnant or lactating. Researchers have demonstrated that antibodies to cows milk can be found in the blood of the umbilical cord, and have found proteins from cows milk in human breast milk[59, 60]. In addition to this, dairy products consumed by a pregnant women increase the level of the growth hormone IGF-1 in her blood that affects the fetus. This can lead to increased birth weight, prescription for diabetes, obesity and overweight, kinds of cancer and celiac disease[61].

Acne and milk

Acne and pimples develops as a result of blockages in follicles, and is characterized by noninflammatory open or closed comedones and by inflammatory papules, pustules, and nodules. Acne affects the areas of skin with the densest population of sebaceous follicles, which includes the face, the upper part of the chest, and the back[72]. Androgen hormones are thought of as the initial trigger[66]. Androgene hormone receptors are present in sebaceous glands, and individuals with malfunctioning androgen receptors do not develop acne[67]. Androgene hormones promote sebum production and release, helping to clog the follicles of the skin[68].

Acne affects 60 to 70 percent of the Western population at some time during their life. Among these 60 to 70 percent, 20 percent has severe acne with permanent physical and mental scarring[62]. Acne is during adolescence, more common in men than in women. But in adulthood, acne is more common in women than in men[63]. 20 percent of women and five percent of men at age 25 has acne. By age 45 years, five percent of both men and women do still have acne[66]. Acne can cause psychosocial suffering, such as reduced self-esteem, and studies have found that acne often can result in depression and suicide[69, 70, 65, 71].

Many dermatologists do not recognize the association between diet and acne, which largely is caused by a poorly conducted study from 1964. The researchers conducting the study in 1964 gave 65 test subjects either chocolate or did not give them chocolate. They compared the acne of the two groups, but did not record what the participant ate and drank beside of chocolate, and therefore found no association between diet and acne[73]. Other studies have found different results, and have shown that acne has a lot to do with the Western diet, and really is just one of many lifestyle diseases which is occurring largely as a result of the Western diet. A team of researchers visited the island Kitavan, New Guinea and the Aché tribe living in Paraguay and find no trace of acne at all. And a physician, who for 30 years have lived and worked among the Eskimo, found no trace of Acne while they ate their natural diet, but as soon as they shifted towards a Western diet, acne became just as common as in is in the Western world. Physicians working on the island Okinawa during World War II found that acne was unknown before the war, but became common as soon as the Western diet came to the island. In the rural areas of Brazil where people still consumed their natural diet, researchers only found acne in 2.7 percent of 9955 children and young adults aged 6 to 16 year studied. And in Pretoria, South Africa only two percent of the subjects studied in a study had acne, compared to 10 percent of the white population which often eats the components of the Western diet[74]. In the American Nurse Study, 47,355 female nurses were quizzed about their diet patterns and about whether they had acne as younger. Here, the researchers conducting the study, found a crystal clear association between dairy products and acne[75].

The same is seen in studies of 4,273 boys and 6,094 girls, that found a clear association between dairy products and acne[76, 77]. Anther study, a study of 4273 individuals sought to examine the association between dietary dairy intake and teenaged acne among boys. The teenage boys reported dietary intake, and those who ate more than two servings of dairy products a day, had compared to those who ate less than one serving of dairy products a day, a 19 percent greater chance of getting acne[78]. Another team of researchers studied 6,094 girls, age 9 to 15 years. Those girls who drank more than one glass of milk a day had 20 to 30 percent more acne than those girls who only drank less than one glass of milk a day. The girls drank low-fat milk to show that it was something else than the fat in the milk, that caused the acne. The researchers suggested that it was the cancer promoting substance, the growth hormone IGF-1, that along with male hormones and androgens was causing the girls acne[79]. Milk do also contain sex steroids which promotes the production of sebum. Beside of this do the IGF-1 promotes the production of sebum, inflammation and cells which closes the comedones. And already before birth can a child be disponeret for acne if its mother consumes large amounts of dairy products. The IGF-1 will affect the fetus and make it produce larger quantities of the cells able to produce sebum, which all will start producing sebum when the child hits puberty[80].

Milk contain animal protein

Long-term studies of rats have shown that rats have double the risk of developing cancer when they consume animal protein such as casein found in milk. Other studies have shown that cancer in rats disappears when they stop consuming animal protein such as casein. The rats in the study were all given a carcinogenic substance to get the cancer started, but the cancer only developed and caused death to the rats that were fed animal protein. In a study over the course of two years were all the rats fed animal protein death at the end of the study, while the rats who were not fed animal protein all lived and where at good health. All of the rats were fed the carcinogenic chemical, aflatoxin. Some of the rats were only fed animal protein the first year of the study, and only consume small amounts of animal protein for the rest of the study. Among these rats, the prevalence of cancer where 35 to 40 percent smaller at the end of the study. The same kinds of studies have been made with mice, several kinds of cancer and other carcinogenic chemicals with the same results. The animal protein in the rats diet propelled the cancer, and the rats eating no animal protein did not develop cancer even though they were fed highly carcinogenic chemicals. This kind of studies have been made at several universities and have been conducted by different researchers, and they have all shown the same[81, 82].

This research have been conducted over the course of several decades and have just recently been collected and presented as a whole. Some researchers and health professionals have criticized the author of many studies and a book showing animal protein as a cancer promoter, T. Colin Campbell, suggesting that animal protein only promotes cancer in the animals tested, rats and mice. But many findings suggest the opposite, and Colin do in his book, The China Study tell an anecdote concerning one of the findings. In the late 1960-ties, Colin worked with a team in the Philippines fighting undernourishment. Peanuts is a good and cheap source of protein, and the American doctors and researchers thought that it was protein the children lagged. But the peanuts were often infected with kinds of fungi that created a carcinogenic chemical called aflatoxsin. The chemical can result in liver cancer, but the most interesting thing was that most of the children with liver cancer in the Philippines lived in wealthy parts of the country. The parts where the population could afford to replace the original healthy and cheap diet of fruit and vegetables, with the Western diet consisting largely of animal protein and fat. So even though the poor population ate the cheap peanuts of poor quality, and the diet with the highest concentration of Aflatoxin, they still suffered much less from liver cancer[83]. A similar example is from Japan, where smoking is much more common than in the US, but Japan do still have much fever cases of lung cancer than do the US. In 1955, 54 percent of the American men smoke and 76 percent of the Japanese men smoke. Some decades later, in 1985, "only" 33 percent of the American men smoke, but 60 percent of the Japanese men smoked in the year 1992. In spite of this did two to three times as many American men die from lung cancer, than did Japanese men in the period. And Japanese men who lives in the US and consume the Western diet, has the same risk of dying from lung cancer, than do men of American origin living in America. This suggest just as before, that diet plays a crucial part in the development of cancer[84].

The amount of growth hormone in the blood and the risk of breast cancer is highly associated. A study showed that women with a high level of growth hormone in the blood, had seven times greater risk of developing breast cancer than did women with a low level of growth hormone in the blood[85]. A study of 25,892 Norwegian women showed that those who consumed more than 7.5 dl milk daily had three times greater risk of developing breast cancer, than those who consumed 1.5 dl milk daily[86]. IGF-1 has also been shown to increase the risk of ovarian cancer, prostate cancer, cancer in the livmoderhals and cancer in the æggestokke[87, 88, 89]. Growth hormone is also known to make children grow faster and make them reach puberty early. American girls do on average has their first period at the age 11 years, while girls living in the rural areas of China have their first period at the age 17 years. This makes the American girls able to get pregnant several years earlier than their Chinese peers, and is thereby exposed to large amounts of estrogen for a longer period of time. Estrogen affects cancers like breast cancer, prostate cancer, cancer in the testicles, and cancer in the female genitals[90].

Milk contains great amounts of fat, unless it is removed. The fat found in milk directly from the cow accounts for 48 percent of the calories found in milk, and the fat in low-fat milk with "only" two percent fat accounts for 34 percent of the calories found in low-fat milk. Fat accounts for 73 percent of the calories found in cheddar cheese, and almost all of the calories in butter come from fat. In comparison do only five calories or the energy found in a banana come from fat, and only one calorie in a baked potato comes from fat(91). Studies suggest that protein from milk triggers the onset of insulin-dependent diabetes in children. Certain children produce antibodies for the protein, which in turn destroy insulin producing cells in the pancreas. A study of 142 children with diabetes, showed that all 142 children had high levels of antibodies for protein found in milk[92].

When humans eat dairy products the level of IGF-1 rises in the body. Studies have shown that a pint of milk a day, results in a ten percent increase in IGF-1 levels among adolescent girls. A similar rise in IGF-1 levels is seen in postmenopausal women consuming three servings of low-fat milk a day[93, 94]. The ability of the cows milk to increase IGF-1 levels is needed in order to make the calf gain a lot of weight over a small amount of time. But in humans, the increased levels of IGF-1 helps cancer growth in the body and speeds up the aging process of the body. Especially prostate cancer, lung cancer, colon cancer and breast cancer growth is promoted by IGF-1[95, 96]. Dairy products are the greatest dietary source of oestrogen, delivering about 60 to 70 percent of all dietary oestrogen. The large amount of oestrogen exists in dairy products because of the cow being milked while it is pregnant in modern factory farms[97, 98]. A high dietary intake of oestrogen has several times been associated with prostate cancer, breast cancer and cancer in the uterus.

Individuals eating the Western diet with large amounts of dairy products and meat have the most cases of osteoporosis worldwide. Countries like America, Denmark, Sweden, Norway the United Kingdoms and New Zealand suffer most cases of osteoporosis, and countries with only a minimal consumption of dairy products, like countries in Asia and Africa have very few cases of osteoporosis[99, 100]. IGF-1 stimulates cells of the body to live longer and inhibits the natural death of old cell occurring in the body. This is a problem when it comes to cancer cells, providing the cancer cells better conditions to provide illness to the body and making it harder to kill the cancer cells[(100)]. IGF-1 makes the body grow old faster because it makes the cells of the body divide faster. IGF-1 makes both healthy cells divide faster, but also sick and defect cells like cancer cells[101]. Studies have shown that mice with a genetic defect that causes lower levels of IGF-1, lives as much as 40 percent longer than mice with a normal level of IGF-1. These mice do also physically speaking look younger and resist diseases better. They do as well have better joints, brains, eyes and immune system[102]. The effect on lifetime and of growth in animals that IGF-1 has, is seen in dogs. Small dogs with lover levels of IGF-1 live longer than large dogs with high levels of IGF-1. Big dogs like Dobermans and Grand Danois have high levels of IGF-1 and do live significant fewer years than small dogs like small terriers and Chihuahuas with low levels of IGF-1. Large dogs live an average of ten years, and small dogs live an average of 13 years[104]. The same is seen in humans where tall individuals live shorter lives than low individuals[105]. Several researchers do also belie that a lowering of activity of IGF-1 in the body is a key element to prolong human lifetime[103]. But the level of IGF-1 in the body can be lowered by consuming a healthy diet based on starches, vegetables and fruit. A study of 292 vegan women living in Great Britain found that they had 13 percent lower IGF-1 activity than the 99 omnivores and 101 vegetarians participating in the study, and other studies have shown a similar effect in vegan men[106, 107].

Fatty acids

Three types of fatty acids are found in food. They are monounsaturated, polyunsaturated and saturated fatty acids, and they exist in varying amounts in food. All fatty acids are organic molecules which consists of long chains of carbon, oxygen and hydrogen atoms. The more saturated a fatty acid is, the more oxygen atoms is attached to the molecule. Saturated fat is found mainly in animal foods like eggs, meat and dairy products. The fat molecules are all stuffed with or "saturated" with hydrogen. This type of fat is most of the time hard at room temperature, and it is linked to the lifestyle diseases of the Western world in countless medical studies. Vegans do rarely need to be afraid of saturated fat since vegan diets are really low in saturated fat. The main exceptions are tropical oils like coconut oil and palm oils. Vegetarians and pescetarians need to be concerned with saturated fat, since dairy, eggs and animal foods of the ocean are loaded with saturated fat.

Different kinds of fatty acids

Monounsaturated Fatty Acids are fatty acids that unlike Saturated Fat, have one carbon atom in the chain without a hydrogen atom linked to it. This makes it saturated one place, or as it is called, monounsaturated. Stored in cold spaces like the refrigerator, Monounsaturated Fatty Acids are partly solid, but most of them become liquid at room temperature. Monounsaturated Fatty Acids are only dangerous if you consume so generous amounts of them that you become overweight or obese, and when they are consumed in the right amounts, they protect against a large amount of diseases. Sources of Monounsaturated Fatty Acids are canola oil, olive oil, nuts, olives, sunflower oil etc.

Polyunsaturated Fatty Acids are molecules of fat with more than one opening in the fat molecule. They are liquid at room temperature and are also liquid when they are stored in the refrigerator. Just as Monounsaturated Fatty Acids, Polyunsaturated Fatty Acids are not dangerous if they are consumed in limited amounts. The main vegetable sources of Polyunsaturated Fatty Acids are seeds, nuts, grains, legumes, vegetables oils and plant foods in general.

Essential Fatty Acids are fatty acids necessary to the body. Two fatty acids are essential – meaning that they are required in the diet in order to make the body function properly. These two fatty acids are Linoleic Acid in the Omega-6 fatty acid family, and the other is Alpha-linolenic Acid in the Omega-3 fatty acid family. Most diets provide 10 times more Omega-6 fatty acids than they provide Omega-3 fatty acids. But Omega-3 fatty acids have in general better nutritional capacities than do Omega-6 fatty acid, why it is a good idea to plan you diet in a way that maximises intake of Omega-3 fatty acids.

Long-Chain Polyunsaturated Fatty Acids are long chains of polyunsaturated fatty acids. They can unlike Essential Fatty Acids be synthesized by the body, but it is still extremely important and healthful to get them from the diet. One way to synthesise Long-Chain Polyunsaturated Fatty Acids is to convert Linoleic Acid to Arachidonic Acid. Another way is to convert Alpha-linolenic fatty acids to Eicosapentaenoic Acid (EPA) and Docosahexaenoic Acid (DHA). Dietary sources of Long-Chain Polyunsaturated Fatty Acids relevant for individuals following a plant based diet is fish and microalgae.

Trans Fatty Acids have a low smelting and boiling point, increase shelf life of foods but are a health disaster even worse than Saturated Fat. They are a type of Monounsaturated Fatty Acid that have been processed and rearranged their atoms. Seen from the eyes of the food industry Trans Fatty Acids are a blessing, but from a health concerned point of view they are something to be entirely avoided. Trans Fatty Acids are extremely rare in the vegan diet but are often seen in the vegetarian and pescetarian diet.

Fat is a neccesary part of the diet

Views on how many percents of the daily need for energy that should be consumed as fat depends on which source you choose to believe in. The debate is quite polarized, with one side believing in high fat diets and the other in low fat diets. Individuals following the Low Fat Vegan Diet consume about 10 to 15 percent of their energy with excellent results. A diet higher in fat, The Mediterranean Diet have also showed good results and have many followers. Individuals following this eating pattern derives about 30 to 40 percent of their energy from fat. The mainstream scientific community recommends that adults gets between 15 and 30 percent of their daily energy as fat. Children between age one and three should consume 30 and 40 percent of their energy as fat and children and young adult between the age four and 18 should get 25 to 35 percent of their daily energy need from fat.

Essential Fatty Acids

Adequate intakes of for Linoleic Acid (LA) is 12 grams daily for women and 17 grams daily for men. The adequate intake of Alpha-linolelic Acid (LNA) is 1.1 grams daily for women and 1.6 grams daily for men. This will provide a ratio of about 10 to 11 units of Omega-6 to 1 unit of Omega-3. These recommendations are meant for individuals who consume some kind of animal food. Recommendations for vegans and near vegans are that the ratio between Omega-6 and Omega-3 should be about 2:1 or 4:1. To achieve this ratio, the amount of energy from Omega-6 fatty acids should be maintained at 5-8 percent of the daily intake of energy and the intake of Omega-3 fatty acids should be raised to between 1.25 and 2.5 percent of the daily calories.

If you are having trouble meeting these needs like most of the omnivorous population supplements can be taken to meet your needs. It is also a good idea to take supplements if you are pregnant, lactating, elderly or have a condition that decreases the ability of your body to convert essential fatty acids into the fatty acids that you need. Just remember not to overuse supplements and other dietary sources of Omega-3 and Omega-6 fatty acid, because the ratio between the two types fatty acids should be right.

Dietary sources of Omega-6 fatty acids are oils and seeds of sunflower, hemp, grape, safflower, sesame, pumpkin, walnuts, butternut, soybeans etc. Omega-3 can be obtained from fatty acids such as dark green leafy vegetables, hemp, flaxseed, chia, canola, butternut, microalgae, fish and eggs.

Essential Fatty Acids metabolism

When the Omega-6 fatty acid, Linoleic Acid (LA) is obtained by the body by eating sunflower, corn, safflower, grapeseed oil, grains or walnuts, it is made into Gamma-linolenic Acid (GLA), which can be obtained from primrose and borage oils. Gamma-linolenic acid is made into Arachidonic Acid (AA), which is then later on made into more powerful eicosanoids, which is also found in animal fat.

Alpha-linolenic Acid (LNA) can be obtained from hemp seed, flaxseed, walnuts, canola oil, greens and butternuts. Alpha-linolenic acid is in the body made into Eicosapentaenoic Acid (EPA), which can be obtained from fish, microalgea and seaweed. This is made into Docosahexaenoic Acid (DHA), which also can be obtained from eggs, fish and microalgae.

Fatty Acid content of some foods

	% calories from fat	% of total fat that is sat. fat	% of total fat that is mono. fat
Oils			
Canola oil, 1 Tbsp.	100	7	61
Corn oil, 1 Tbsp.	100	13	29
Cottonseed oil, 1 Tbsp.	100	26	22
Flaxseed oil, 1 Tbsp.	100	9	18
Grapeseed oil, 1 Tbsp.	100	5	16
Hempseed oil, 1 Tbsp.	100	8	16
Olive oil, 1 Tbsp.	100	15	75
Palm oil, 1 Tbsp.	100	51	39
Palm kernel oil, 1 Tbsp.	100	85	11
Peanut oil, 1 Tbsp.	100	19	48
Safflover oil, 1 Tbsp.	100	6	14
Safflover oil, high oleic, 1 Tbsp.	100	6	75
Sesame oil, 1 Tbsp.	100	14	40
Soybean oil, 1 Tbsp.	100	14	23
Sunflower oil, 1 Tbsp.	100	10	19
Sunflower oil, high oleic, 1 Tbsp.	100	10	84
Walnut oil, 1 Tbsp.	100	9	23
Nuts, seeds and soy			
Almonds, 1 oz.	80	10	65
Butternuts, 1 oz.	84	2	18
Cashews, 1 oz.	72	20	59
Flaxseed, whole, 2 Tbsp.	41	9	18
Flaxseed, ground, 2 Tbsp.	41	9	18
Hazelnuts, 1 oz.	87	7	75
Macadamia nuts, 1 oz.	95	16	78
Peanuts, 1 oz.	76	14	50
Pecans, 1 oz.	94	8	59

% of total fat that is Omega-6 fat	% of total fat that is Omega-3 fat	LNA (g)	EPA (mg)	DHA (mg)
21	11	1.6	0	0
57	0	0	0	0
52	0	0	0	0
16	57	8.0	0	0
70	0	0	0	0
57	19	2.7	0	0
9	1	0.8	0	0
10	0	0	0	0
2	0	0	0	0
33	0	0	0	0
75	0	0	0	0
14	0	0	0	0
42	0	0	0	0
51	7	0.9	0	0
65	0	0	0	0
4	0	0	0	0
53	13	1.7	0	0
23	1	0.14	0	0
59	15	2.5	0	0
17	0	0	0	0
16	57	5.2	0	0
16	57	3.8	0	0
14	0	0	0	0
2	0	0	0	0
32	0	0	0	0
26	1	0.3	0	0

	% calories from fat	% of total fat that is sat. fat	% of total fat that is mono. fat
Pistachios, 1 oz.	72	12	53
Pumpkin seeds, 1 oz.	76	19	31
Soybeans, 1 cup cooked	47	14	22
Firm tofu, 1/2 cup	54	14	22
Walnuts, 1 oz.	90	6	14
Seaweeds			
Irish moss, 100 g, raw	< 1	32	14
Kelp, 100 g, raw	12	63	25
Spirulina, 100 g, raw	13.5	49	12
Wakame, 100 g, raw	13	32	14
Fruits and vegetables			
Avocado, 1 medium	86	16	63
Greens, 1 cup	12-14	28	5
Olives, 10 large	84	13	74
Animal foods			
Egg, 1 large	61	31	38
High-fat fish, 3 oz.	40 - 50	20	50
Low-fat fish, 3 oz.	5 - 10	20	20

% of total fat that is Omega-6 fat	% of total fat that is Omega-3 fat	LNA (g)	EPA (mg)	DHA (mg)
30	0	0	0	0
45	0-5	0 - 0.7	0	0
50	7	1.0	0	0
50	7	0.7	0	0
58	14	2.6	0	0
7	45	0.001	0.001	0
18	2	0.004	0.004	0
23	15	0.2	0.2	0
8	46	0.001	0.001	0
12	1	0.25	0	0
11	56	0.1	0	0
8	0.5	0.02	0	0
12	0.7	0.02	5	51
2	23	0.1	500	800
6	50	0	100	150

So, what should i actualy eat?

An effective way of keeping track of what you eat, is to measure the foods in the "unit," servings.

6 to 11 servings of **grains** could be eaten daily.
Each of the following counts as a serving:
1 slice of bread; 1 oz. (28 g) of cereal; 1/2 cup of cooked grains; cereal and pasta; 2 Tbsp. of wheat germ; 1 oz. (28 g) of grains products.

3 or more servings of **vegetables** could be eaten daily.
Each of the following counts as a serving:
1/2 cup (120 ml.) vegetables; 1 cup (240 ml.) salad; 3/4 cup (180 ml.) vegetable juice.

2 or more servings of **fruit** could be eaten daily.
Each of the following counts as a serving:
1/2 cup (120 ml.) of fruit; 3/4 (180 ml.) fruit juice

2 to 3 servings of **bean** products could be eaten daily:
Each of the following counts as a serving:
1 cup (240 ml.) cooked legumes; 1/2 cup (120 ml.) of tofu or tempeh; 1 serving of veggie meat like a burger or wiener; 3 Tbsp. (45 ml.) of nut or seed butter; 1/4 cup (60 ml.) of nuts or seeds; 2 cups (480 ml.) of soy milk.

6 to 8 servings of **high calcium foods** could be consumed daily.
Each of the following counts as a serving:
1/2 cup (120 ml.) fortified soymilk; 1/4 cup (60 ml.) calcium-set tofu; 1/2 cup (120 ml.) of calcium fortified orange juice; 1/4 cup (60 ml.) almonds; 3 Tbsp. (45 ml.) almond butter; 1 cup (240 ml.) cooked, or 2 cups (480 ml.) raw, of high calcium leafy green vegetables; 1 cup (240 ml.) high calcium beans; 1/4 cup (60 ml) dry hijiki seaweed; 1 Tbsp (15 ml.) blackstrap molasses; 5 figs.

Beside of this should you consume one or two servings of essetial **omega-3 fatty acid** foods. One serving is either 1 tsp. flax oil; 4 tsp. canola oil; 3 Tbsp. walnuts.

Dietary supplements of **Vitamin B12** needs to be taken to ensure adequate intake, if you don't have access to fortified foods. Daily intake of Vitamin B12 should be 2.4 micrograms for adults, 2.6 to 2.8 if you are pregnant or lactating and 0.9 to 1.8 micrograms for children.

Dietary supplements of **Vitamin D** is also needed if you live in cold areas of the world or spend most of your time indoor. Sunshine, dietary supplements or fortified foods should add up to 5 microgram daily for children, young adults and adults, 10 micrograms daily for individuals older than 51, and 15 micrograms daily for people older than 70 years of age.

You should aim at drinking 6 to 8 glasses of water and other fluids daily, and the best source of fluids is water directly from the tap.

It is also important to get exercise, and about one hour of physical activity daily should help to keep your body healthy.

A vide variarity of foods from all of the food groups should be consumed. This helps the body to obtain a vide variarity of vitamins, psytochemicals, nutrients and fiber.

Highly concentrated fats and oils are often poor sources of nutrients why it only should be consumed in small amounts. The same thing should be said about refined carbohydrates like glucose.

The following pages contains examples of what an american registered dietritian would recommend you to consume daily.

1,600 calorie menu

1,600 calories a day could be appropriate for individuals trying to loose weight, are quite small, handicapped, inactive or for individuals who are older than adult and therefore less mobile.

Food group	Breakfast	Lunch
Food eaten	Cereal with soymilk and fruit	Lentil soup, crackers, vegetables with dip / dressing, and fruit
Grains	1 cup/240 mL cooked cereal or 2 oz./ 60 g other grain product	3 rice cakes or crackers
Vegetables		2 cups / 480 mL raw carrots, celery, peppers, cherry, tomatoes, cucumper
Fruit	1/2 cup / 120 mL berries or other fruit	1 slice watermelon or 1 other fruit
Bean and bean alternates	1 cup / 240 mL fortified soymilk	1 cup / 240 mL cooked lentils in lentil soup
Fortified soymilk and alternates	1 cup / 240 mL fortified soymilk	
Other essentials		

Dinner	Snack	Number of servings from each food group
Stir fried green, tofu and rice	Banana shake and pop-corns	
1 cup / 240 mL cooked brown rice or other grain	3 cup	6
1 cup / 480 mL broccoli, 1 cup / 240 mL chinese greens stirred fried		4
	1 banana	3
1/4 cup / 60 mL firm tofu	1 cup /240 mL fortified soymilk	2 1/2
1/4 cup / 60 mL tofu, 1 cup / 240 mL broccoli and Napa cabbage	1 cup / 240 mL fortified soymilk	7
Supplements of Vitamin B12 and one omega-3 serving		1

2,200 calorie menu

1,600 calories a day could meet the needs of most active children, women, teenage girls and men who are less active.

Food group	Breakfast	Lunch
Food eaten	Cereal with soymilk and fruit	Vegetable soup and pita bread filled with hummus
Grains	1 cup/240 mL cooked cereal or 2 oz./ 60 g other grain product	2 pita bread
Vegetables		1 cups / 240 mL vegetable soup
Fruit	3/4 cup / 180 mL juice or one piece of fruit	
Bean and bean alternates	1 cup / 240 mL fortified soymilk	1 cup / 240 mL of hummus without oil
Fortified soymilk and alternates	1 cup / 240 mL fortified soymilk	1 cup / 240 mL of hummus without oil
Other essentials		

Dinner	Snack	Number of servings from each food group
Tofu and grain or rolls, green salad, dressing	Soymilk, figs, or almonds	
1 cup / 240 mL cooked grains or two small rolls	3 cup	6
4 cup / 960 mL salad containing 2 cup / 480 mL calcium rich greens		6
		1
4 oz. / 120 g firm tofu		2 1/2
4 oz. / 120 g firm tofu, 2 cup / 480 mL leafy green vegetable in salad	1/2 cup / 120 mL fortified soymilk, 2 figs, or 1/4 cup / 60 mL almonds	7
Supplements of Vitamin B12 and one omega-3 serving		1

2,500 calorie to 2,800 calorie menu

1,500 calories to 2,800 calories a day could meet the needs of most very active women, active men and teenage boys.

Food group	Breakfast	Lunch
Food eaten	Cereal, soymilk, fruit, toast with butter and blackstrap molases	Vegetable club sandwich andsoy milk
Grains	2 slices toast, 1 cup/240 mL whole grain cereal or 2 oz. / 60 g dry cereal	3 slices whole grains bread
Vegetables		Slices of tomato, and lettuce
Fruit	One piece of fruit	1 cup / 240 mL soy milk
Bean and bean alternates	2 Tbsp / 30 mL almond butter and 1 cup / 240 mL soymilk	6 slices veggie bacon and veggie turkey
Fortified soymilk and alternates	2 tsp blackstrap molasses, 2 Tbsp / 30 mL almond butter	1 cup / 240 mL soy milk
Other essentials		

Dinner	Snack	Number of servings from each food group
2 veggie burgers or baked beans	Figs and walnuts	
		7
		5 1/2
	5 figs	4
2 veggie burgers or a large serving of baked beans	3 Tbsp / 45 mL walnuts	6
	5 figs	7
Supplements of Vitamin B12	Walnuts 3 Tbsp / 45 mL (one omega-3 serving)	1

4,000 calorie menu

4,000 calories a day could meet the needs of most athletes, men who work hard jobs, or the needs of individuals trying to gain weight.

Food group	Breakfast	Lunch
Food eaten	Cereal with soymilk, bagels with tahini and jam, soy milk	2 vegan burgers and fruit
Grains	2 bagels or 3 slices of toast and 1 cup / 240 mL cereal	2 rolls
Vegetables		tomato slices and lettuce
Fruit		2 pieces of fruit
Bean and bean alternates	1 1/2 cup / 360 mL soy milk and 3 Tbsp / 45 mL sesame tahini	2 vegan burgers
Fortified soymilk and alternates	1 1/2 cup / 360 mL soy milk and 3 Tbsp / 45 mL sesame tahini	
Other essentials		

Dinner	Snack	Number of servings from each food group
Stir fried tofu, cahew and vegetables with rice or noodles	Fruit shake, granola bar, walnuts, raisins and soy milk or soy yogurt	
2 cup / 480 mL brown rice or noodles	1 cup / 240 mL granola	13
Vegetables including leafy green vegetables		4 1/2
	2 Tbsp / 30 mL raisins	7
1/4 cup / 60 mL cashew and 1/4 cup / 60 mL tofu	1 cup / 240 mL soy milk or soy yogurt	7
1/4 cup / 60 mL tofu	1/2 cup / 120 mL soymilk	8
Supplements of Vitamin B12 and one omega-3 serving	3 Tbsp / 45 mL walnuts (1 omega-3 serving)	1

Plant eater and athlete

A simple browse of Wikipedia will show that many successfully athletes follows vegan or vegetarian diets. Both athletes training for an Ironman or athletes training for the swimming Olympics can prosper and achieve their maximum on a plant based diet. Many athletes do even become vegan solely because they want to achieve better physically. The energy needed to fuel a vegan or vegetarian athlete varies with the size of the body, the gender, weight and various other factors concerning the athlete. Physical activity does often increase the energy need and basal metabolic rate by as much as 30 percent, whereas somewhat more energy is needed. The energy need of the body is different for the hobby athlete exercising an hour three times a week, than for the professional athlete exercising many hours daily. The body tends to be very good at informing you on how much energy you need, and when you become more active will the body begin to crave more food providing energy.

Needs of athletes

Most athletes should not eat more than a maximum of 6,000 calories a day, and most athletes should not consume so many calories, but still relatively more than standard white collar workers, working in office jobs. In order to consume a large dose of energy from plant based sources, it is normally necessary to eat foods high in energy like tofu, seeds, shakes, nuts and butters. Mainstream sources recommends that about 60 to 70 percent of the energy consumed by an athlete should come from carbohydrates. The consumption of carbohydrates fills up glycogen stores in the body, making you able to work harder and work for a longer period of time before becoming exhausted. In order to fill glycogen depots in the muscles, vegan athletes should consume about 6 to 8 grams of carbohydrates per kilo body weight. This high intake of carbohydrates should mainly come from whole sources like fruits, legumes, vegetables, whole grains and nuts. This will insure a high intake of vitamins, antioxidants and psychochemical's, helping the body to perform good at athletic events. Except for the day of the sport event and the days prior to it, refined carbohydrates like sugar should only constitute a maximum of 10 percent of the carbohydrate intake.

Protein should amount to about 12 to 15 percent of the daily energy consumption for individuals performing athletic. Protein does only contribute three to six percent of the energy fuelling vegan athletes that want to perform the highest. The general rule is that the more calories you consume as carbohydrates, the lesser calories is needed from protein. Carbohydrate intake does always serve as the limiting factor when it comes to muscle deposition. An athlete training for the Ironman, and who therefore have extraordinary high calorie intake should aim at getting about 15 percent of the daily calories from protein, while an endurance athlete should aim at consuming about 12 percent of his or her daily calories as protein. It should not be necessary to consume protein powder and protein bars in order to get enough protein, if you just plan your diet appropriately. Too much protein can be consumed, and if too much protein is eaten it do pose a danger to the health of the body and its organs. It is not common for individuals following a plant based diet to get so much protein that it poses a danger, but it can happen for individuals eating protein supplements like protein shakes and bars and also eats highly concentrated and processed protein rich foods like soyburgers and soywieners. Eating excess protein will not increase muscle mass of improve performance, but it will pose a danger to the kidneys and other organs and the overall health.

Fat is a major source of energy and provides about 75 percent of the energy used by the body during distance events, being burned after the glycogen stored in the muscles is used. Fat is stored many places in the body, both within muscles ready to be burned and to be used as ready energy, and as fat stores around the body's cells where it can fuel athletic performance over longer time. Unlike carbohydrates, fat can be stored over longer spaces of time and do not need to be replenished if it is not used. The amount of fat athletes should consume depends on how much energy they consume as carbohydrates and protein. Dietary fat intake should not be higher than 30 percent of the daily calories and a dietary intake of 25 percent should be appropriate for most athletes.

Eating plants and weighing too much

If you consume more energy than you use you are likely to gain weight and will eventually end up overweight or obese. As a vegan or a vegetarian you are much less likely to consume more energy than you eat, because your diet contains just the right amount of energy you need and fills up a lot more space than the traditional Western diet. Shifting to a vegan diet is a great way to lose weight and to stay at a healthy weight when you have lost those damaging and unnecessary kilos of body-fat.

What constitutes overweight?
The most used and easy way to determine whether you are underweight, normalweight, overweight or obese is the Body Mass Index (BMI). It can be used to calculate an estimate of the weight state of your body, if you are not pregnant, a child, nursing or have really big muscles like a body builder.

Body Mass Index is calculated by using the following formula:
$BMI = weight/height^2$
The height should be measured in meter (m) and the weight should be measured in kilograms (kg).
- BMI less than 18.5 means that you are underweight
- BMI between 18.5 and 25 means that you are normalweight
- BMI between 25 and 30 means that you are overweight
- BMI more than 30 means that you are obese

The most accurate way of measuring overweight and obesity is by measurement of body-fat. A body-fat percentage greater than 17 percent in men and 27 percent in women means that you are overweight, and a body-fat percentage greater than 25 percent in men and 31 percent in women means that you are obese.

A way to control weight

Vegetarian and especially Vegan diets often contains more fibre and fewer calories per kilogram of food eaten. More fibre means that you are consuming a lot of food volume that provides very few calories to your diet. It makes your feel full, filling up space that would otherwise had been filled up by food containing calories and helps speed food through youre digestive system. Vegan and vegetarian diets contain more complex carbohydrates that speed up the metabolic rate, making you burn of more calories per unit of time. Vegan and vegetarian diets also contains less fat, and fat have more than twice as many calories per unit of weight than do protein and carbohydrates. It would be a good idea to aim for six to seven servings of grain products daily. Whole grains should be chosen, being more slowly digested than refined grains. Unrefined whole grains like brown rice, barley, millet and quinoa should be chosen over whole grain bread, cereal and pasta. Refined grains like white pasta and bread, white rice and other highly refined grain products should be totally avoided. Vegetables should be eaten about three or more servings daily because they offer the most nutrients for the least calories. This means that you can eat generous amounts without eating more than a moderate amount of calories. Raw vegetables tend to fill up even more space than cooked ones, and some research suggests that a part of the nutrients found in vegetables gets lost when they are heated. Fruit contains almost no fat, and about six servings of fruit should be eaten daily. Leafy green vegetables are the source of calcium with the lowest portion of fat, and is therefore the easiest way to meet your calcium needs without consuming too much energy. Fruit juice should not substitute fruit as they are found in nature, and it is generally a good idea to consume different kinds of fruits because they contain different kinds of nutrients. Whole legumes are as whole grain better than refined ones. Whole legumes contain less fat, than nuts and their butters. Beside of the low fat percentage, whole sources of legumes contain as whole sources of grains large amounts of fibre which makes you feel full earlier.

Eating plants and not weighing enough

Just as being overweight mainly is about consuming more calories than you use, underweight is about eating fewer calories than you use. Other causes of underweight are diseases such as cancer and other things that can be wrong with your body. From the section of overweight, you know that Body Mass Index (BMI) can be used as a tool to determine which class of weight you are in. Underweight individuals have a Body Mass Index of less than 18.5. Body Mass Index can only serve as an indicator of whether you are underweight, and it is often you're body that tells you whether you are underweight. Underweight individuals are often in the underweight BMI section and are in a poor state of health. They do often need a long time to recover from disease, are often sick and lags energy. Individuals with a Body Mass Index that suggest they are underweight could also be normalweight individuals with light bones, just as normalweight individuals could be underweight individuals with heavy bones.

Narcotic substances like alcohol, cigarettes and drugs can interfere with your metabolic system and interfere with your weight. Cutting all kinds of narcotic substances will often help you gain weight, and narcotic substances are in no way healthful for you. If you are trying to gain weigh, you should try and limit your time spent exercising to a maximum of an hour three times a week. As written, you can only gain weight corresponding to the amount of calories you are not burning off exercising and training for your Ironman. In order to gain weight, you will need to add about 500 to 1,000 calories to your diet daily. This should be enough to add one or two pounds to your weight weekly. To eat this amount of calories, you will need to add some fat to your diet and, or consume larger portions of what you normally consume

The following is a list of some of the sources i have used in the making of this book. Some have i red, and others have i just had my hands on.

Litterature used for "The perils of dairy" chaptor:
1 - Henrietta Fleck, Introduction to Nutrition, 4th ed. New York: Macmillan, 1981.
2 - Ældste danske kogebog – Forlaget Wormianum, 2002)
3 - Suhr, 1 ; Mad – grundkogebog og køkkenskole – Gads Forlag 1994
4 - Omtalt i Hyldtoft , O. (red), 2009: Kost og spisevaner i 1800-tallet
5 - Dansk mælkebog p. 101)
6 - http://www.dyrenes-beskyttelse.dk/docs/maelkeydelse d. 9. juli 2010)
7 - USDA APHIS. "DAIRY CATTLE". Retrieved 2009-05-29)
8 - Lands, William E.M. (1 May 1992). "Biochemistry and physiology of n–3 fatty acids". FASEB Journal (Federation of American Societies for Experimental Biology) 6 (8): 2530–2536. PMID 1592205. Retrieved 2008-03-21.)
9 - Lands, William E.M. (December 2005). "Dietary fat and health: the evidence and the politics of prevention: careful use of dietary fats can improve life and prevent disease". Annals of the New York Academy of Sciences (Blackwell) 1055: 179–192. doi:10.1196/annals.1323.028. PMID 16387724.)
10 - Hibbeln, Joseph R.; N; B; R; L (June 1, 2006). "Healthy intakes of n–3 and n–6 fatty acids: estimations considering worldwide diversity". American Journal of Clinical Nutrition (American Society for Nutrition) 83 (6, supplement): 1483S–1493S. PMID 16841858)
11 - Simopoulos, A.P.2002: The importance of the ratio of omega-6/omega-3 essential fatty acids. Biomed. Pharmacother.56(8) 365-79)
12 - Daley, C.A.; Abbott, A.; Doyle, P.; Nader, G.; and Larson, S. (2004). A literature review of the value-added nutrients found in grass-fed beef products. California State University, Chico(College of Agriculture). Retrieved 2008-03-23.
13 - Simopoulos, Artemis P. (October 2002). "The importance of the ratio of omega-6/omega-3 essential fatty acids". Biomedicine & Pharmacotherapy 56 (8): 365–379. doi:10.1016/S0753-3322(02)00253-6. PMID 12442909)
14 -Heini, A.F. & Weinsier, R.L. 1997: Divergent trends in obesity and fat intake. The american paradox. American Journal of Medicine 102(3) 259-264
15 - XXX)
16 - Dansk mælkebog)
17 - Malekinejad, H. et al. 2006: Naturally Occuring Estrogens in Processed Milk and in Raw Milk (from Gestated Cows). J. Agri. Food Chemistry 54 9785-9791
18 - Field, R. A., M. L. Riley, et al. (1974). Bone Composition in Cattle, Pigs, Sheep and

Poultry. Journal of Animal Science 39(3): 493-499.
19 - Legros, R., N. Balmain, et al. (1987). Age-Related-Changes in Mineral of Rat and Bovine Cortical Bone. Calcified Tissue International 41(3): 137-144.
20 - http://www.denstoredanske.dk/Natur_og_milj%C3%B8/Biokemi_og_molekyl%C3%A6rbiologi/Biokemi/parathyreoideahormon d. 9. juli 10
(21 - Hypponen, E. et al. 2001: Intake of vitamin D and risk of type 1 diabetes: a birth-cohort study. Lancet 358, 1500-1503.)
22 - Rostand, S.G. 1979: Ultraviolet light may contribute to geographic and racial blood pressure differences. Hypertension 30, 150-156.)
23 - Kraise, R. et al. 1998: Ultraviolet B and blood pressure. Lancet 352, 709-710.)
24 - Swagery, D.L. et al. 2002: Lactose intolerance. American Family Physician 65 (9) 1845-50)
25 - U.S. Department of Health and Human Services 2004 Bone Health and Osteoporosis: A Report of the Surgeon General. U.S. Department of Health and Human Services, Office of the Surgeon General, Rockville, MD, USA.)
26 - Riggs BL, Melton LJ III 1995 The worldwide problem of osteoporosis: Insights afforded by epidemiology. Bone 17(Suppl):505S–511S.)
27 - Chrischilles EA, Butler CD, Davis CS, Wallace RB 1991 A model of lifetime osteoporosis impact. Arch Intern Med 151:2026–2032.)
28 - Cummings SR, Melton LJ 2002 Epidemiology and outcomes of osteoporotic fractures. Lancet 359:1761–1767.)
29 - WHO Scientific Group 2003 Prevention and management of osteoporosis. World Health Organ Tech Rep Ser 921:1–9. 6. Tucker KL, Hannan MT, Kiel DP 2001 The acid-base hypothesis: Diet and bone in the Framingham Osteoporosis Study. Eur J Nutr 40:231–237.
30 - Abelow B. Cross-cultural association between dietary animal protein and hip fracture: a hypothesis. Calcific Tissue Int 50:14-8, 1992.)
31 - Frassetto LA . Worldwide incidence of hip fracture in elderly women: relation to consumption of animal and vegetable foods. J Gerontol A Biol Sci Med Sci. 2000 Oct;55(10):M585-92.)
32 - Remer T. Influence of diet on acid-base balance. Semin Dial. 2000 Jul-Aug;13(4):221-6.)
33 - Frassetto L. Diet, evolution and aging--the pathophysiologic effects of the post-agricultural inversion of the potassium-to-sodium and base-to-chloride ratios in the human diet. Eur J Nutr. 2001 Oct;40(5):200-13.)
34 - Barzel US. Excess dietary protein can adversely affect bone. J Nutr. 1998 Jun;128(6):1051-3.)

35 - Protective Effect of Total Carotenoid and Lycopene Intake on the Risk of Hip Fracture: A 17-Year Follow-Up From the Framingham Osteoporosis Study. Shivani Sahni,1 Marian T. Hannan,2 Jeffrey Blumberg,3 L. Adrienne Cupples,4 Douglas P. Kiel,2 and Katherine L. Tucker1. J Bone Miner Res. 2009 June; 24(6): 1086–1094.

36 - Maurer M. Neutralization of Western diet inhibits bone resorption independently of K intake and reduces cortisol secretion in humans. Am J Physiol Renal Physiol. 2003 Jan;284(1):F32-40.

37 - Peter J. Nijweidi, E. H. B., AND JEAN H. M. FEYEN (1986). "Cells of Bone: Proliferation, Differentiation, and Hormonal Regulation." Physiological Reviews 66(4): 855-886

38 - Arnett, T. 2003: Regulation of bone cell function by acid-base balance. Proc. Nutr. Soc. 62, 511-20

39 - XXX

40 - Remer, T. et al. 2003: Dietary potential acid load and renal net acid excretion in healthy, free living children and adolescents. American Journal of Clinical Nutrition 77, 1255-60

41 - Frasetto L.A. et al. 2000: Worldwide Incidence of Hip Fracture in Elderly Women: Relation to Consumption of Animal and Vegetable Foods. J. Geront. 55A, 585-592.

42 - Breslau, N.A. 1988: Relationship of animal-protein rich diet to idney stone formationand calcium metabolism. Clin. Endocrinol. Metab. 66, 140-46.

43 - Delvecchio FC. Medical management of stone disease. Curr Opin Urol. 2003 May; 13(3): 229-33.

44 - Tucker KL, Hannan MT, Kiel DP 2001 The acid-base hypothesis: Diet and bone in the Framingham Osteoporosis
Study. Eur J Nutr 40:231–237.

45 - Prynne CJ, Mishra GD, O'Connell MA, Muniz G, Laskey
MA, Yan L, Prentice A, Ginty F 2006 Fruit and vegetable intakes and bone mineral status: A cross sectional study in 5 age and sex cohorts. Am J Clin Nutr 83:1420–1428.

46 - Tucker KL, Chen H, Hannan MT, Cupples LA, Wilson PW, Felson D, Kiel DP 2002 Bone mineral density and dietary patterns in older adults: The Framingham Osteoporosis Study. Am J Clin Nutr 76:245–252.

47 - Macdonald HM, New SA, Golden MH, Campbell MK, Reid DM 2004 Nutritional associations with bone loss during the menopausal transition: Evidence of a beneficial effect of calcium, alcohol, and fruit and vegetable nutrients and of a detrimental effect of fatty acids. Am J Clin Nutr 79:155–165.

48 - Tucker KL, Hannan MT, Chen H, Cupples LA, Wilson PW, Kiel DP 1999 Potassium, magnesium, and fruit and vegetable intakes are associated with greater bone mineral density in elderly men and women. Am J Clin Nutr 69:727–736.

49 - New SA, Bolton-Smith C, Grubb DA, Reid DM 1997 Nutri- tional influences on

bone mineral density: A cross-sectional study in premenopausal women. Am J Clin Nutr 65:1831–1839.

50 - Chen Y, Ho S, Lee R, Lam S, Woo J 2001 Fruit intake is associated with better bone mass among Hong Kong Chinese early postmenopausal women. J Bone Miner Res 16:S1;S386.

51 - Macdonald H, Downie F, More F, New S, Grubb D, Reid D 2001 Higher intakes of fruit and vegetables are associated with higher bone mass in perimenopausal Scottish women. Proc Nutr Soc 60:202A.

52 - New SA, Robins SP, Campbell MK, Martin JC, Garton MJ, Bolton-Smith C, Grubb DA, Lee SJ, Reid DM 2000 Dietary influences on bone mass and bone metabolism: Further evidence of a positive link between fruit and vegetable con- sumption and bone health? Am J Clin Nutr 71:142–151.

53 - Mælkebog p. 13

54 - Høst, A. et al. 2002: Clinical course of cow's milk protein allergy/intolerance and atopic diseases in childhood. Pedist. Allergy Immunol. 13 Suppl. 15:23-8.

55 - Le Berre, N &Queinnec, H. 2009: Soyons moins lait. Terre Vivante.

56 - Benhamou, A.H. et al. 2009: An overview of cow's milk allergy in children. Swiss Med. Weekly. 139 (21-22) 300-307.

57 - Pelto, L. et al. 1998: Milk hypersensitivity – key to poorly defined gastrointestinal symptoms in adults. Allergy 53, 307-310.

58 - Le Berre. N. 1990: Le Lait Une sacrée vacherie? Editions Charles Corlet.

59 - Akcadus, M. et al. 2006: The relationship among intrauterine growth, insuline-like growth factor 1 (IGF-1), IGF-1 binding protein-3, and bone mineral status in newborn enfants. Am. J. Perinatol. 23, 473 – 480.

60 - Maeda, S. et al. 1993: The concentration of bovine IgG in human breast milk measured using different methods. Acta Pediatritian. 82, 1012-1016.

61 - Melnik, B. 2009: Milk consumption: aggravating factor of acne and promotor of chronic diseasis of Western societies. Journ. Germ. Soc. Derm. 7 364-370.

62 - Fulton JE, Black E. Dr. Fulton's Step-by-Step Program for Clearing Acne. New York, NY: Harper & Row; 1983

63 - Shaw JC, White LE. Persistent acne in adult women. Arch Dermatol. Sep 2001;137(9):1252-3.

64 - Kligman AM. Postadolescent acne in women. Cutis. Jul 1991;48(1):75-7

65 - Mulder MM, Sigurdsson V, van Zuuren EJ, et al. Psychosocial impact of acne vulgaris. evaluation of the relation between a change in clinical acne severity and psychosocial state. Dermatology. 2001;203(2):124-30.

66 - Thiboutot D, Gilliland K, Light J, Lookingbill D. Androgen metabolism in sebaceous

glands from subjects with and without acne. Arch Dermatol. Sep 1999;135(9):1041-5.
67 - Holland DB, Cunliffe WJ, Norris JF. Differential response of sebaceous glands to exogenous testosterone. Br J Dermatol. Jul 1998;139(1):102-3.
68 - Pochi PE, Strauss JS. Sebaceous gland activity in black skin. Dermatol Clin. Jul 1988;6(3):349-51.
69 - Purvis D, Robinson E, Merry S, Watson P (December 2006). Acne, anxiety, depression and suicide in teenagers: a cross-sectional survey of New Zealand secondary school students. J Paediatr Child Health 42 (12): 793–6.
70 - Goodman G (July 2006). "Acne and acne scarring - the case for active and early intervention" (PDF). Aust Fam Physician 35 (7): 503–4.
71 - Picardi A, Mazzotti E, Pasquini P (March 2006). "Prevalence and correlates of suicidal ideation among patients with skin disease". J Am Acad Dermatol 54 (3): 420–6.)
72 - Simpson, Nicholas B.; Cunliffe, William J. (2004). "Disorders of the sebaceous glands". in Burns, Tony; Breathnach, Stephen; Cox, Neil; Griffiths, Christopher. Rook's textbook of dermatology(7th ed.). Malden, Mass.: Blackwell Science. pp. 43.1–75. ISBN 0-632-06429-3.)
73 - Fulton, J.E. et al. 1964: Effect of chocolate on acne vulgaris. JAMA 210 (11) 2071 – 1074)
74 - Cordain, L et al. 2002: Acne Vulgaris. A disease of western civilization. Arch. Dermatol. 138 1584 – 1590.
75 - Adebamowo, C.A. et al. 2005: High school dietary dairy intake and teenage acne. J. Am. Acad. Dermatol. 52(2) 207-793.
76 - Adebamowo, C.A. et al. 2008: Milk consumption and acne in teenage boys. J. Am. Acad. Dermatol. 58(5) 787-793
77 - Adebamowo, C.A. et al. 2006: Milk consumption and adolescent in teenage girls. Dermatology online journal 07/11.
78 - Milk consumption and acne in teenaged boys. Clement A. Adebamowo, Donna Spiegelman, Catherine S. Berkey, William Danby, Helaine H. Rockett, Graham A. Colditz, Walter C. Willett, Michelle D. Holmes. Volume 58. Issue 5, Pages 787-793 (May 2008).
http://www.eblue.org/article/S0190-9622(07)02402-4/abstract
79 - Adebamowo CA, Spiegelman D, Berkey CS, Danby FW, Rockett HH, Colditz GA, Willett WC, Holmes MD. Milk consumption and acne in adolescent girls. Dermatol Online J. 2006 May 30;12(4):1.
80 - Melnik, B. 2009: Milk consumption: aggravating factor of acne and promotor of chronic diseasis of Western societies. Journ. Germ. Soc. Derm. 7 364-370.
81 - MgBodile, M.U.K & Campbell, T.C. 1972: Effect of protein deprivation of male weaning rats. Journal of Nutrition 102. 53-609

82 - Youngman, L.D. & Campbell, T.C. 1992: Inhibition of aflatoxin B1-induced gamma-glutamyl... Carcinogenisis 13, 1607-1613

83 - Campbell, T.C. & Campbell T.M. 2006: The China Study, Benbella.)

84 - Stellman, S.D. et al. 2001: Smoking and Lung Cancer Risk in American and Japanese Men. Cancer epidemiology 10, 1193-1199.

85 - Hankinson, S.E. et al 1998: Circulation concentration of insulin-like growth factor-1 and risk of breast cancer. The Lancet 351 (9113) 1393-96.

86 - Gaard, M. et al 1995: Dietary fat and the risk of breast cancer. Int. Journ. Cancer 63 16-17.

87 - Druckmann, R. 2002: IGF-1 in gyneacology and obstetrics. Maturitas 41 suppl. 1 65-83.

88 - Roddam, A.W. et al 2008: Insulin-like growth factors, their binding proteins and prostate cancer risk. Ann. intern. Med 149 (7) 461-471.

89 - Gunnel, D.J. 2003: Are diet prostate-cancer associations mediated by the IGF axis? British J. Cancer 88, 1682-1686.

90 - Gao, X 2005: Prospective sudies of dairy products and calcium intake and prostate cancer. Journ. Natl. Cancer. Inst. 97, 1768-1777

91 - Journal of the American Dietetic Association. Volume 95, Number 6 (June, 1995)

92 - H.C. Gerstein, "Cow's Milk Exposure and Type 1 Diabetes Mellitus," diabetes Care (1993) 17:13-19.

93 - Cadogan J, Eastell R, Jones N, Barker ME. Milk intake and bone mineral acquisition in adolescent girls: randomised, controlled intervention trial. BMJ. 1997 Nov 15;315(7118):1255-60.

94 - Heaney RP, McCarron DA, Dawson-Hughes B, Oparil S, Berga SL, Stern JS, Barr SI, Rosen CJ. Dietary changes favorably affect bone remodeling in older adults. J Am Diet Assoc. 1999 Oct;99(10):1228-33.

95 - Moschos SJ, Mantzoros CS. The role of the IGF system in cancer: from basic to clinical studies and clinical applications. Oncology. 2002;63(4):317-32.

96 - Rincon M, Rudin E, Barzilai N. The insulin/IGF-1 signaling in mammals and its relevance to human longevity. Exp Gerontol. 2005 Nov;40(11):873-7.

97 - Sharpe R. Are oestrogens involved in falling sperm counts and disorders of the male reproductive tract?Lancet 341:1392, 1993.

98 - Janowski T. Mammary secretion of oestrogens in the cow. Domest Anim Endocrinol. 2002 Jul;23(1-2):125-37.

99 - Abelow B. Cross-cultural association between dietary animal protein and hip fracture: a hypothesis. Calcific Tissue Int 50:14-8, 1992.

100 - Frassetto LA . Worldwide incidence of hip fracture in elderly women: relation to consumption of animal and vegetable foods. J Gerontol A Biol Sci Med Sci. 2000

Oct;55(10):M585-92.9
101 - Bartke A, Chandrashekar V, Dominici F, Turyn D, Kinney B, Steger R, Kopchick JJ. Insulin-like growth factor 1 (IGF-1) and aging: controversies and new insights. Biogerontology. 2003;4(1):1-8.
102 - Miller RA. Genetic approaches to the study of aging. J Am Geriatr Soc. 2005 Sep;53(9 Suppl):S284-6.
103 - Holzenberger M. The GH/IGF-I axis and longevity. Eur J Endocrinol. 2004 Aug;151 Suppl 1:S23-7.
104 - Life expectancy of dogs: http://www.pets.ca/pettips/tips-46.htm
105 - amaras TT, Elrick H, Storms LH. Is height related to longevity? Life Sci. 2003 Mar 7;72(16):1781-802.
106 - Allen NE, Appleby PN, Davey GK, Kaaks R, Rinaldi S, Key TJ. The associations of diet with serum insulin-like growth factor I and its main binding proteins in 292 women meat-eaters, vegetarians, and vegans. Cancer Epidemiol Biomarkers Prev. 2002 Nov;11(11):1441-8.
107 - Allen NE, Appleby PN, Davey GK, Key TJ. Hormones and diet: low insulin-like growth factor-I but normal bioavailable androgens in vegan men. Br J Cancer. 2000 Jul;83(1):95-7.

Litterature used for the "Carbohydrates" chaptor:

- American Diabetes Association. Nutrition recommendations and principles for people with diabetes mellitus. Diabetes Care 1994; 17: 519-22.
- Anderson J W, Smith BM and Gustasson J. The practicality of high fibre diets. Am J Clin Nutr 1994; 59(supp):1242S-47S.
- Cassidy A., Bingham, S.A., Cummings, J.H. Starch intake and colorectal cancer risk: an international comparison. British Journal of Cancer 1994; 69:937-42.
- Cummings JH, Macfarlane GT. The control and consequences of bacterial fermentation in the human colon. Journal of Applied Bacteriology 1991; 70:443-59.
- Davies GJ. Dietary fibre intakes of individual with different eating patterns. Hum Nutr Appl Nutr 1985; Apr;39(2):139-48.
- Foster-powell K and Brand Miller J. International tables of glycemic index. Am J Clin Nutr 1995; 62:871S- 93S.
- Harland BF and Morris ER Phytate: good or bad food component? Nutrition Research 1995; Vol.15.No.5:733- 754.
- Holt, S., Brand Miller, J.C., Petcoz, P. Relationships between satiety and plasma glucose and insulin responses to foods. Proceedings of the Nutrition Society of Australia 1996; 20:177.

- Jacobs DR, Slavin J and Marquart L. Whole grain intake and cancer; a review of the literature. Nutrition and Cancer 1995; 24: 221-9.
- Livesey G. Metabolizable energy of macronutrients. Am J Clin Nutr 1995; 62 (suppl):1135S-42S.
- Mackay S and Ball M J. Do beans and oatbran add to the effectivness of a low fat diet? Europ J Clin Nutr. 1992; 46:641-648.
- Okano, G., Sato, Y., Takumi, Y., Sugawara, M. Effect of pre-exercise high carbohydrate and high fat meal ingestion on endurance performance and metabolism. International Journal of Sports Medicine 1996; 17:530- 534.
- Spencer H, Norris C, Durlar J, et al. Effect of oatbran on calcium absorption and calcium, phosphorus, magnesium balance in men. J Nutr 1991; 121:1976-1983.
- Stephen, A.M., Sieber, G.M., Gerster, Y.A., Morgan, D.R. Intake of carbohydrate and its components - international comparisons, trends over time and effects of changing to low fat diets. Am J Clin Nutr 1995;62:851S-67S.
- The Joint FAO/WHO Expert Consultation on Carbohydrates in Human Nutrition, April 1997.

Litterature used fot the "Minerals" chaptor:

- Gibson R, Anderson BM, and Sabry JH. The trace mineral status of a group of postmenopausal vegetarians. J. Amer. Diet. Assoc. 1983;82(3):246-250.
- Gibson R Content and bioavailability of trace elements in vegetarian diets. Am. J. Clin. Nutr. 1994 59: 1223S- 1232S.
- Groff JL, Gropper SS, Hunt SM. Advanced Nutrition and Human Metabolism. West Publishing Co, St Paul MN, 1995.
- Kramer L, Osis D, Coffey J, Spencer H. Mineral and trace element content of vegetarian diets. J. Am. Coll. Nutr. 1984;3 (1)3-11.
- Messina MJ, Messina VL. The Dietitian's Guide to Vegetarian Diets: Issues and Applications. Gaithersburg, MD: Aspen Publishers; 1996.
- Position of The American Dietetic Association: Vegetarian Diets. J. Amer. Diet. Assoc. 1997; 97(11):1317- 1321.
- Rosado, JL, Lopez P, Morales M, Munoz E, Allen LH. Bioavailability of energy, nitrogen, fat, zinc, iron and calcium from rural and urban Mexican diets. British J. Nutr. 1992; 68:45-8.
- Subcommittee on the 10th Edition of the RDAs, Food and Nutrition Board, Commission on Life Sciences, National Research Council. Recommended Dietary Allowances. 10th ed. Washington, DC: National Academy Press; 1989.

- The Report of the Scientific Review Committee. Nutrition Recommendations. Health and Welfare Canada, 1990
- Traber, M, The bioavailability bugaboo. Am J Clin Nutr 2000 71: 1029-1030
- Yates A, Schlicker S and Suitor C. Dietary Reference Intakes; The new basis for recommendations for calcium and related nutrients, B vitamins and choline. J. Amer. Diet. Assoc. 1998;98:(6):699-705.
- Alaimo et al, Dietary intake of vitamins, minerals and fiber of persons ages 2 months and over in the United States: Third National health and - Nutrition Examination Study, Phase 1, Number 258, National Center for Health Statistics, November 1994.
- Anderson, John JB Plant-based diets and bone health: nutritional implications. Am. J. Clin. Nutr.1999 70: 539S- 542S.
- Dibba B, Prentice A, Ceesay M, Stirling D M, Cole TJ, Poskitt EM. Effect of calcium supplementation on bone mineral accretion in Gambian children accustomed to a low-calcium diet. Am. J. Clin. Nutr. 2000 71: 544-549.
- Do vegetarians need less? Update on calcium. Vegetarian Nutrition Health Letter, Loma Linda University, Loma Linda, CA. vegletter@sph.llu.edu 1999;2(2):1-3,8.
- Eaton, B, Nelson D. Calcium in evolutionary perspective Am.. J. Clin. Nutr., 281S-287S, 1991
- Eliott RB, Harris DP, Hill JP, Bibby NJ, Wasmuth HE, Type I (insulin-dependent) diabetes mellitus and cow milk:casein varian consumption. Diabetologia 1999;42(3):292-6
- Flatz, G, Genetics of lactose digestion in humans, Ch. 1 in Advances in Human Genetics, edited by Harry Harris and Kurt Hirschhorn, Plenum Press, NY, 1987.
- Fleming KH, Heimbach JT. Consumption of calcium in the US: food sources and intake levels. 1994;J.Nutr. 124:1426S-1430S.
Gueguen, L, Pointillart A, The bioavailability of dietary calcium. J. Amer. Coll. Nutr, 2000;19 (2):119S-136S.
- Guillemant J, Le H-T, Accarie C, Tézenas du Montcel S, Delabroise A-M, Arnaud M and Guillemant S. Mineral water as a source of dietary calcium: acute effects on parathyroid function and bone resorption in young men. Am J Clin Nutr 2000 71: 999-1002
- Heaney, R, Calcium: how your diet affects requirements, Vegetarian Nutrition Health Letter 1(3):1-2, 1998. Heaney, R. Calcium Lecture, in Vancouver/Burnaby, Canada, April 26, 1999
- Heaney R, M, Dowell S, Rafferty K, and Bierman J. Bioavailability of the calcium in fortified soy imitation milk, with some observations on method. Am J Clin Nutr 2000 71: 1166-1169
- Heaney, R. There should be a dietary guideline for calcium. Am. J. Clin.. Nutr. 2000;71(3), 658-661
- Hu JF, Zhao XH, Jia JB, Parpia B, Campbell TC. Dietary calcium and bone density

among middle-aged and elderly women in China. Am. J. Clin.. Nutr. 1993 58: 219-227.
- Itoh R, Nishiyama N, and Suyama Y. Dietary protein intake and urinary excretion of calcium: a cross- sectional study in a healthy Japanese population. Am. J. Clin. Nutr. 1998 67: 438-444.
- Lau EM, Kwok T, Ho SC. Bone mineral density in Chinese elderly. Eur. J. Clin Nutr. 1998;52(1):60-64.
- McDowell et al, Energy and macronutrient intake of vitamins, minerals and fiber of persons ages 2 months and over in the United States: Third National health and Nutrition Examination Study, Phase 1, Number 255, National Center for Health Statistics, November 1994
- Montgomery RK, Buller HA, Edmond H, Rings HM, Grand RJ. Lactose intolerance and the genetic regulation of intestinal lactase-phlorizin hydrolase. The FASEB Journal 1991;5:2824
- Munger RG, Cerhan JR, Chiu BC. Prospective study of dietary protein intake and risk of hip fracture in postmenopausal women. Am. J. Clin. Nutr. 1999 69: 147-152.
- Munger, Ronald G, James R Cerhan and Brian C-H Chiu Prospective study of dietary protein intake and risk of hip fracture in postmenopausal women, Am.. J. Clin.. Nutr.. Vol. 69, No. 1, 147-152, January 1999.
- New, S , Simon P Robins, Marion K Campbell, James C Martin, Mark J Garton, Caroline Bolton-Smith, David A Grubb, Sue J Lee and David M Reid Dietary influences on bone mass and bone metabolism: further evidence of a positive link between fruit and vegetable consumption and bone health? Am.. J. Clin. Nutr. 2000;71(1)142- 151.
- Simoons, F. The geographic hypothesis and lactose malabsorption: a weighing of the evidence. Digestive Diseases. 1978;23 (11):963-980.
- Tucker, Katherine L, Marian T Hannan, Honglei Chen, L Adrienne Cupples, Peter WF Wilson and Douglas P Kiel Potassium, magnesium, and fruit and vegetable intakes are associated with greater bone mineral density in elderly men and women. Am. J. Clin. Nutr., 1999;Vol. 69, No. 4, 727-736, April
- Yates, A.A,. Schlicker, S.A, Suitor, C.W., Dietary reference intakes: the new basis for recommendations for calcium and related nutrients, B vitamins and choline, J. Amer. Dietet Assoc. 98(6);699-705, 1998
- Weaver, CM., Proulx, W. R. and Heaney, R Choices for achieving adequate dietary calcium with a vegetarian diet. Am.. J. Clin. Nutr. 1999;70(3)543S-548S, September
- Weaver, CM., Plawecki K. Dietary calcium: adequacy of a vegetarian diet. Am.. J. Clin. Nutr. 1994;59:1238S- 41S.
- Alexander D, Ball MJ, Mann J Nutrient intake and haematological status of vegetarians and age-sex matched omnivores. Eur. J. Clin. Nutr. 1994;48(8):538-46.
- Ball MJ. Bartlett MA. Dietary intake and iron status of Australian vegetarian women.

Am.. J. Clin. Nutr. 70(3):353-8, 1999.
- Barton JC, et al. Management of hemochromatosis. Annals of Internal Medicine. 1998;129:932-939.
- Beard J, Iron: a balancing act. Vegetarian Nutrition Health Letter 1998;1(4)1-3.
- Cook JD. Adaptation in iron metabolism. Am. J. Clin. Nutr. 1990;51:301-8.
- Freeland-Graves J, Mineral adequacy of vegetarian diets. Am. J. Clin.. Nutr.1988;48:859-62.
- Gibson R, Donovan U, Heath A, Dietary strategies to improve the iron and zinc nutriture of young women following a vegetarian diet. Plant Foods for Human Nutrition, 1997;51:1-16
- Gleerup A, Rossander-Hulthen L, Gramatkovski E, Hallberg L.Iron absorption from the whole diet. Am.. J. Clin. Nutr. 1995;61, 97-104.
- Haddad EH, Berk LS, Kettering JD, Hubbard RW, Peters WR. Dietary intake and biochemical, hematologic, and immune status of vegans compared with nonvegetarians American Journal of Clinical Nutrition, 1999;70(3): 586S-593S.
- Hallberg L, Hulthén L. Prediction of dietary iron absorption: an algorithm for calculating absorption and bioavailability of dietary iron. Am J Clin Nutr 2000 71: 1147-1160
- Hambraeus L, Animal and plant-based diets and iron status; benefits and costs. Proc. Nutr. Soc. 1999;58:235- 42.
- Hunt JR, Roughead ZK. Adaptation of iron absorption in men consuming diets with high or low iron availability
- Kannan S, Factors in vegetarian diets influencing iron and zinc bioavalability. Issues in Vegetarian Dietetics. 1998;VII (3) Spring:1, 7-8.
- Looker AC, Dallman PR, Carroll MD, Gunter EW, Johnson CL. Prevalence of iron deficiency in the United States. J.A.M.A. 1997 Mar 26;277(12):973-6
. Reddy M, Hurrell R, and Cook J. Estimation of nonheme-iron bioavailability from meal composition Am J Clin Nutr 2000 71: 937-943
Sanders T, The nutritional adequacy of plant-based diets. Proc Nutr. Soc. 1999;58(2)265-9.
- Wilson AK, Ball MJ Nutrient intake and iron status of Australian male vegetarians Eur J Clin Nutr 1999 Mar;53(3):189-94.
- Xue-Cun C et al, Low levels of zinc in hair and blood, pica, anorexia and growth in Chinese preschool children. Am.. J. Clin. Nutr.. 1985;42:694-700.
- Zhu TI, Haas JD, Response of serum transferrin receptor to iron supplementation in iron-depleted, nonanemic women. Am. J. Clin.. Nutr. 1998;67:271-5.
- Zinc in Vegetarian Diets. Vegetarian Nutrition Health Letter, Loma Linda University, Loma Linda, CA. vegletter@sph.llu.edu 1999;2(7):1-2,7
Iodine

- Are vegetarians an 'at risk' group for iodine deficiency? British Journal of Nutrition (1999), 81, 3-4.
- Lightowler HJ, Davies GJ.Iodine intake and iodine deficiency in vegans as assessed by the duplicate-portion technique and urinary iodine excretion" British Journal of Nutrition (1998), 80, 529-535
- Phaneuf D, Cote I, Dumas P, Ferron LA, LeBlanc A Evaluation of the contamination of marine algae (Seaweed) from the St. Lawrence River and likely to be consumed by humans. Environ Res 1999 Feb;80(2 Pt 2):S175-S182
- Remer T. Neubert A. Manz F. Increased risk of iodine deficiency with vegetarian nutrition. British Journal of Nutrition (1999;81:45-49
- Butcher M, Judd P, Cayhill CP, Peach S, Diplock AT. Current selenium content of foods and an estimation of average intake in the United Kingdom. Proc. Nutr. Soc. 1995;54(suppl):131A.
- Judd P, Long A, Butcher M, Cayhill CP, Diplock AT. Vegetarians and vegans may be most at risk from low selenium intakes. British Medical Journal. 1997;314(7097)1834
- Schultz TD, Leklem JE. Selenium status of vegetarians, nonvegetarians and hormone dependent cancer subjects. Am. J. Clin.. Nutr. 1983;37:114-118.
- Kaplan N, The dietary guideline for sodium: should we shake it up? No. Am J Clin Nutr 2000 71: 1020-1026.
- McCarron, D The dietary guideline for sodium: should we shake it up? Yes! Am J Clin Nutr 2000 71: 1013- 1019
- Sodium and health. Vegetarian Nutrition Health Letter, Loma Linda University, Loma Linda, CA. vegletter@sph.llu.edu 2000;3(2)1-3.

Litterature used for the "Eating plants and performing athletic" chaptor:

- Wolinsky E and Driskell JA (eds) Sports Nutrition: Vitamins and Trace Elements. Boca Raton: CRC Press, 1997.
- Zachwieja J. Influence of muscle glycogen depletion on the rate of resynthesis. Med Sci Sports Exer 1991; 23:44-48.
- American College of Sports Medicine Position Stand: Exercise and fluid replacement. Med. Sci. Sports Exerc. 28: i-vii.
- American College of Sports Medicine. Position statement: the recommended quantity and quality of exercise for developing and maintaining cardiorespiratory and muscular fitness in healthy adults. Med Sci Sports Exer 1990; 22: 265-274.
- Nieman DC. Vegetarian dietary practices and endurance performance. - Am J Clin Nutr 1988; Sep;48(3 Suppl):754-61.

- Nieman, DC. Physical fitness and vegetarian diets: is there a relation? Am J Clin Nutr 1999; Sep;70(3 Suppl):570S-575S.
- Otis CL, Drinkwater B, Hohnson M et al. ACSM Position Stand on the Female Athlete Triad. Med Sci Sports Exer 1997; 29(5): 1-9.
- Wood PD. Exercise and lipids. Am J Sports Med 1996; 24(6 Suppl): S59-60.
- American Dietetic Association. Nutrition for physical fitness and athletic performance for adults - Position of ADA and the Canadian Dietetic Association J Am Diet Assoc 1993;93:691-697.
- Armsey TD Jr., Green GA. Nutrition supplements: science vs hype. The Physician and Sportsmedicine 1997; V25, No. 6: 77-92.
- Barr, SI. Vegetarianism and menstrual cycle disturbances: is there an association? Am J Clin Nutr 1999 70(suppl):549-554S.
- Cheuvront, SN. The zone diet and athletic performance. Sports Med. 1999 Apr;27(4):213-28.
- Dorfman L. The Vegetarian Sports Nutrition Guide. John Wiley and Sons, New York, 2000.
- Gatorade Sports Science Institute. Web site: http://www.gssiweb.com/ Gatorade Sports Science Institute. Muscle Builder Supplements: RT#37. 1999; Vol. 10, No. 3. Web site: http://www.gssiweb.com/
- Gatorade Sports Science Institute. Nutritional Supplements for strength trained athletes: SSE#47. 1993; Vol. 6, No. 6. Web site: http://www.gssiweb.com/
- Gatorade Sports Science Institute. Nutritional Supplements for weight gain: SSE#68. 1998; Vol. 11, No. 1. Web site: http://www.gssiweb.com/
- Groff JL, Gropper SS, Hunt SM. Advanced Nutrition and Human Metabolism. West Publishing Co, St Paul MN, 1995.
- Hawley JA, Dennis SC, Lindsay FH, Noakes TD. Nutritional practices of athletes: are they sub-optimal? J Sports Sci 1995; Summer;13 Spec No:S75-81.
- Hargreaves, Mark. Metabolic Response to Carbohydrate Ingestion: Effects on Exercise Performance, 12th Annual Gatorade Sports Science Conference.
- Holt WS Jr. Nutrition and athletes. Am Fam Physician 1993; Jun;47(8):1757-64.
- Houtkooper L. Food selection for endurance sports. Medicine and Science in Sports and Exercise 1992; Suppl: 349S-359S.
- Koshy, K.M., E. Griswold, and E.E. Schneeberger. Interstitial nephritis in a patient taking creatine. N Eng J Med 1999; 340:814-15.
- Lemon PW. Is increased dietary protein necessary or beneficial for individuals with a physically active lifestyle? Nutr Rev 1996; Apr;54(4 Pt 2):S169-75.
- Messina M, Messina V, The Dietitians Guide to Vegetarian Diets, Gathersburg MD, Aspen Publishers; 1996.

- Raben A, Kiens B, Richter EA, Rasmussen LB, Svenstrup B, Micic S and Bennett P. Serum sex hormones and endurance performance after a lacto-ovo vegetarian and a mixed diet. Med Sci Sports Exerc 1992; Nov;24(11):1290-7.

Litterature used for the "Eating plants and not weighing enough" chaptor:
- Gatorade Sports Science Institute. Nutritional Supplements for weight gain: SSE#68. 1998; Vol. 11, No. 1.
- Maughan RJ. Creatine supplementation and exercise performance. Int J Sport Nutr 1995; V 5, No. 2: 94-101.
- Mujika I, Padilla S. Creatine supplementation as an ergogenic aid for sports performance in highly trained athletes: a critical review. Int J Sports Med 1997; 18: 491-496.
- Armsey TD Jr., Green GA. Nutrition supplements: science vs hype. The Physician and Sportsmedicine 1997; V25, No. 6: 77-92.
- Dawson B, Cutler M, Moody A, Lawrence S, Goodman C and Randall N. Effects of oral creatine loading on single and repeated maximal short sprints. Aust J Sci Med Sport 1995; 27: 56-61.
- Dorfman L. The Vegetarian Sports Nutrition Guide. John Wiley and Sons, New York, 2000.
- Haddad EH, Berk LS, Kettering JD, Hubbard RW, Peters WR. Dietary intake and biochemical, hematologic, and immune status of vegans compared with nonvegetarians American Journal of Clinical Nutrition, 1999; 70(3): 586S-593S.
- Gatorade Sports Science Institute. Web site: http://www.gssiweb.com/
- Gatorade Sports Science Institute. Muscle Builder Supplements: RT#37. 1999; V 10, No. 3. Web site: http://www.gssiweb.com/
- Gatorade Sports Science Institute. Nutritional Supplements for strength trained athletes: SSE#47. 1993; Vol. 6, No. 6. Web site: http://www.gssiweb.com/
- National Institutes of Health: National Hear, Lung and Blood Institute. Clinical guidelines on the identification, evaluation and treatment of overweight and obesity in adults. The Evidence Report. 1998.
- National Institutes of Health: Weight-control Information Network, Web site: www.niddk.nig.gov/health/nutrit/win.htm
- World Health Organization. The World Health Report 1998. http://www.who.int/whr/1998/whr-en.ht

Litterature used for the "Eating plants and weighing too much" chap-

tor:
- American Dietetic Association. Position of the American Dietetic Association: weight management. JADA 1997; 97(1): 71-74.
- American Dietetic Association. Send fat diets packing. January 1999, ADA web site www.eatright.org
- Alfieri M; Pomerleau J, Grace DN. A comparison of fat intake of normal weight, moderately obese and severely obese subjects. Obes Surg 1997; V7, No. 1: 9-15.
- Appleby PN, Thorogood M, Mann JI, Key TJ. Low body mass index in non meat eaters: the possible roles of animal fat, dietary fibre and alcohol. Int J Obes Relat Metab Disord 1998; V 22, No. 5: 454-460.
- Baer DJ, Rumpler WV, Miles CW, Fahey GC Jr. Dietary fiber decreases the metabolizable energy content and nutrient digestibility of mixed diets fed to humans. J Nutr 1997; V 127, No. 4: 579-86.
- Blundell Je, Lawton CL, Hill AJ. Mechanisms of appetite control and their abnormalities in obese patients. Horm Res 1993; Vol 39(suppl 3): 72-76.
- Brown et al. State of the World 2000. Worldwatch Institute, Washington DC, 1999. (visit the Worldwatch website at: www.world watch.org)
- Brownell K D Personal Responsibility and control over our bodies: when expectation exceeds reality. Health Psychology 1991;10(5):303-310.
- Cheuvront, SN. The zone diet and athletic performance. Sports Med. 1999 Apr;27(4):213-28.
- Daly ME, Vale C, Walker M, Alberti KG and Mathers JC. Dietary carbohydrates and insulin sensitivity: a review of the evidence and clinical implications. Am J Clin Nutr 1997; 66(5): 1072.
- Delargy HJ, O'Sullivan KR, Fletcher RJ, Blundell JE. Effects of amount and type of dietary fibre (soluble and insoluble) on short-term control of appetite. Int J Food Sci Nutr 1997; V 48, No. 1: 67-77.
- National Institutes of Health. Gastric surgery for severe obesity. Publication No. 96-4006, 1996.
- National Institutes of Health. Very low-calorie diets. Publication No. 95-3894, 1995.
- Eades MR. Protein Power. Bantam Books, 1996.
- Foreyt JP and Goodrick K. Weight management without dieting. Nutr Today 1993; March/April, pp. 4-9.
- Harvey-Berino J. The efficacy of dietary fat vs. total energy restriction for weight loss. Obes Res 1998; V 6 No. 3: 202-207.
- Health and Welfare Canada. Canadian Guidelines for Healthy Weights. Report of an Expert Group convened by Health Promotion Directorate, Health Services and Promo-

tion Branch. Minister of Supply and Services, 1988.
- Khouzam Skelton N and Skelton W. Medical implications of obesity. Postgraduate Medicine 1992; 92(1):151- 162.
- Kuczmarski RJ, Carrol MD, Flegal KM and Troiano RP. Varying body mass index cutoff points to describe overweight prevalence among U.S. adults: NHANES III (1988-1994). Obes Res 1997; 5:542.
- Levin N, Rattan , Gilat T. Energy intake and body weight in ovo-lacto vegetarians. J Clin Castroenterol 1986; V 8, No 4: 451-53.
- Ludwig DS, Majzoub JA, Al-Zahrani A, Dallal GE, Blanco I and Roberts SB. High glycemic index foods, overeating , and obestiy. Pediatrics 1999; V 103, No. 3: E26.
- Marniemi J, Seppanen A, Hakala P. Long-term effects on lipid metabolism of weight reduction on lactovegetarian and mixed diet. Int J Obes 1990; V 14, No. 2: 113-125.
- McNutt, K. Fat traps, tips and tricks. Nutr Today 1992; May/June:47-49.
- National Institutes of Health: National Hear, Lung and Blood Institute. - Clinical guidelines on the identification, evaluation and treatment of overweight and obesity in adults. The Evidence Report. 1998.
National Institutes of Health: Weight-control Information Network, Web site: www.niddk.nig.gov/health/nutrit/win.htm
- Reaven GM Syndrome X. Clin Diab 1994; 12:32.
- Reaven GM. Do high carbohydrate diets prevent the development or attenuate the manifestations (or both) of syndrome X? a viewpoint stronly against. Curr Opin Lipidol 1997; 8(1): 23.
- Rolls BJ and Hill JO. Carbohydrates and Weight Management. International Life Sciences Institute. ILSI Press, Washington DC, 1998.
- Sears B. Enter the Zone. Harper Collins, 1995. Steward HL, Morrison CB, Andrew SS, Balart LA. Sugar Busters. Ballantine Books, 1998.
- Tiwary CM, Ward JA, Jackson BA. Effect of pectin on satiety in healthy US Army adults. J Am Coll Nutr 1997; Vol 16 No. 5: 423-8.
- Toth MJ, Poehlman ET. Sympathetic nervous system activity and resting metabolic rate in vegetarians. Metabolism 1994; V 43, No. 5: 621-5.
- World Health Organization. The World Health Report 1998. Web site: http://www.who.int/whr/1998/whr- en.htm

Litterature used for the "Protein" chaptor:

- Appleby, PN, Thoroughgood M, Mann, JI and Key T, The Oxford Study: an overview. Amer. J.Clin, Nutr, 1999 (suppl):525S-31S
- Ball D, Maughan RJ. Blood and urine acid-base status of premenopausal omnivorous

and vegetarian women. British Journal of Nutrition. 1997;8(5):683-93.
- ESHA The Food Processor Nutritional Analysis Program
Messina M, Messina V, The Dietitians Guide to Vegetarian Diets: Issues and Applications, Chapter 3 and Appendix A. Gathersburg MD, Aspen Publishers; 1996
- Millward, J. Meat or wheat for the next millenium? The nutritional value of plant-based diets in relation to human amino acid and protein requirements. Proceedings of the Nutrition Society 1999;58:249-260.
- Report of Joint FAO/WHO Expert Consultation, Protein Quality Evaluation, Food and Nutrition Paper 51, FAO of the United Nations, 1991
- Pennington, JA. Bowes and Church's Food Values of Portions Commonly Used. 16th ed. JB Lippincott Co, Philadelphia 1994.
- Protein in Vegetarian Diets. Vegetarian Health Letter, Loma Linda University, Loma Linda CA vegletter@sph.llu.edu 1998;1(7):1-3
- USDA Nutrient Database for Standard Reference at http://www.nal.usda.gov/fnic/cgi-bin/nut_search.pl

Litterature used for the "Older than adult" chaptor:
- American Dietetic Association Manual of Clinical Dietetics, Vegetarian Nutrition chapter, 2000 Baik H, and Russell R. B12 Deficiency In The Elderly. Annu. Rev. Nutr.. 19:357-377. 1999
- Carmel R, Cobalamin, the stomach, and aging. American Journal of Clinical Nutrition, 66:750-759, 1997.
- Carmel R, Green R, Jacobsen D, Rasmussen K, Florea M and Azen C, Serum cobalamin, homocysteine, and methylmalonic acid concentrations in a multiethnic elderly population: ethnic and sex differences in cobalamin and metabolite abnormalities. American Journal of Clinical Nutrition, Vol. 70, No. 5, 904-910.
- Houston D, Johnson M, Nozza R, Gunter E, Kelly J, Cutler G M, Edmonds J. Age-related hearing loss, vitamin B-12, and folate in elderly women. American Journal of Clinical Nutrition; 69(3) 564-571.
- Kort, W. Effect of aging. Nutrition Reviews. 58(3):S19-S21 Lichtenstein, A; Van Horn, L. Very Low Fat Diets, Circulation, Volume 98(9).September 1, 1998.935-939.
- Messina M, Messina V, The Dietitians Guide to Vegetarian Diets: Issues and Applications, Gathersburg MD, Aspen Publishers; 1996
- Papas A, Niessen L, Chauncey H. Geriatric Dentistry: Aging and Oral Health, Mosby Year Book,1991
- Potter S, Baum J, Teng H, Stillman R, Shay N and Erdman J, Soy protein and iso-

flavones: their effects on blood lipids and bone density in postmenopausal women. American Journal of Clinical Nutrition 68:1375S-1379S.
- Rosenburg IH. Nutrition in the elderly Nutr Rev:50;349-350, 1992
- Ryan C, Eleazer P, Egbert J. Vitamin D in the elderly. An overlooked nutrient. Nutrition Today. 1995;30:228- 233. 1995.
- Sciffman S, Moss J, Erickson R. Thresholds of food odors in the elderly. Exp Aging Res, 1976;2:389-398.
- Starling R, Ades P, Poehlman E. Physical activity, protein intake, and appendicular skeletal muscle mass in older men Am J Clin Nutr 1999;70:91-96.
- The Seventh-day Adventist Dietetic Association. Nutrition for Vegetarian/Vegan Seniors, pages 7-1 to 7-7 in
The Vegetarian/Vegan Resource (An Annex to Diet Manuals 1997-1998). Adventist Health. Roseville, CA. 1997.
- Ubbink J. Metabolic markers of vitamin nutritional status. American Journal of Clinical Nutrition, 70: 5, 789- 790, 1999.
- (Editorial) A Healthy Diet: The Fountain of Youth? Vegetarian Nutrition Health Letter, Loma Linda University, Loma Linda, CA. vegletter@sph.llu.edu 1999;2(8)1-4.
- Willett W. Convergence of philosophy and science: the third international congress on vegetarian nutrition. American Journal of Clinical Nutrition. 70(3 Suppl):434S-438S, 1999 Sep.
- Yates A, Schlicker S and Suitor C. Dietary Reference Intakes; The new basis for recommendations for calcium and related nutrients, B vitamins and choline. J. Amer. Diet. Assoc. 1998;98:(6):699-705.

Litterature used for the "Eating plants and not weighing enough" chaptor:

- Armsey TD Jr., Green GA. Nutrition supplements: science vs hype. The Physician and Sportsmedicine 1997; V25, No. 6: 77-92.
- Dawson B, Cutler M, Moody A, Lawrence S, Goodman C and Randall N. Effects of oral creatine loading on single and repeated maximal short sprints. Aust J Sci Med Sport 1995; 27: 56-61.
- Dorfman L. The Vegetarian Sports Nutrition Guide. John Wiley and Sons, New York, 2000.
- Haddad EH, Berk LS, Kettering JD, Hubbard RW, Peters WR. Dietary intake and biochemical, hematologic, and immune status of vegans compared with nonvegetarians American Journal of Clinical Nutrition, 1999; 70(3): 586S-593S.

- Gatorade Sports Science Institute. Nutritional Supplements for weight gain: SSE#68. 1998; Vol. 11, No. 1. Web site: http://www.gssiweb.com/
- Maughan RJ. Creatine supplementation and exercise performance. Int J Sport Nutr 1995; V 5, No. 2: 94-101.
- Mujika I, Padilla S. Creatine supplementation as an ergogenic aid for sports performance in highly trained athletes: a critical review. Int J Sports Med 1997; 18: 491-496.
- National Institutes of Health: National Hear, Lung and Blood Institute. Clinical guidelines on the identification, evaluation and treatment of overweight and obesity in adults. The Evidence Report. 1998.
- National Institutes of Health: Weight-control Information Network, Web site: www.niddk.nig.gov/health/nutrit/win.htm
- World Health Organization. The World Health Report 1998. http://www.who.int/whr/1998/whr-en.htm

Litterature used for the "Eating plants and weighing too much" chaptor:

- American Dietetic Association. Position of the American Dietetic Association: weight management. JADA 1997; 97(1): 71-74.
- American Dietetic Association. Send fat diets packing. January 1999, ADA web site www.eatright.org
- Alfieri M; Pomerleau J, Grace DN. A comparison of fat intake of normal weight, moderately obese and severely obese subjects. Obes Surg 1997; V7, No. 1: 9-15.
- Appleby PN, Thorogood M, Mann JI, Key TJ. Low body mass index in non meat eaters: the possible roles of animal fat, dietary fibre and alcohol. Int J Obes Relat Metab Disord 1998; V 22, No. 5: 454-460.
- Baer DJ, Rumpler WV, Miles CW, Fahey GC Jr. Dietary fiber decreases the metabolizable energy content and nutrient digestibility of mixed diets fed to humans. J Nutr 1997; V 127, No. 4: 579-86.
- Blundell Je, Lawton CL, Hill AJ. Mechanisms of appetite control and their abnormalities in obese patients. Horm Res 1993; Vol 39(suppl 3): 72-76.
- Brown et al. State of the World 2000. Worldwatch Institute, Washington DC, 1999. (visit the Worldwatch website at: www.world watch.org)
- Brownell K D Personal Responsibility and control over our bodies: when expectation exceeds reality. Health Psychology 1991;10(5):303-310.
- Cheuvront, SN. The zone diet and athletic performance. Sports Med. 1999 Apr;27(4):213-28.
- Daly ME, Vale C, Walker M, Alberti KG and Mathers JC. Dietary carbohydrates and

insulin sensitivity: a review of the evidence and clinical implications. Am J Clin Nutr 1997; 66(5): 1072.
- Delargy HJ, O'Sullivan KR, Fletcher RJ, Blundell JE. Effects of amount and type of dietary fibre (soluble and insoluble) on short-term control of appetite. Int J Food Sci Nutr 1997; V 48, No. 1: 67-77.
- National Institutes of Health. Gastric surgery for severe obesity. Publication No. 96-4006, 1996.
- National Institutes of Health. Very low-calorie diets. Publication No. 95-3894, 1995.
- Eades MR. Protein Power. Bantam Books, 1996.
- Foreyt JP and Goodrick K. Weight management without dieting. Nutr Today 1993; March/April, pp. 4-9.
- Harvey-Berino J. The efficacy of dietary fat vs. total energy restriction for weight loss. Obes Res 1998; V 6 No. 3: 202-207.
- Health and Welfare Canada. Canadian Guidelines for Healthy Weights. Report of an Expert Group convened by Health Promotion Directorate, Health Services and Promotion Branch. Minister of Supply and Services, 1988.
- Khouzam Skelton N and Skelton W. Medical implications of obesity. Postgraduate Medicine 1992; 92(1):151- 162.
- Kuczmarski RJ, Carrol MD, Flegal KM and Troiano RP. Varying body mass index cutoff points to describe overweight prevalence among U.S. adults: NHANES III (1988-1994). Obes Res 1997; 5:542.
- Levin N, Rattan , Gilat T. Energy intake and body weight in ovo-lacto vegetarians. J Clin Castroenterol 1986; V 8, No 4: 451-53.
- Ludwig DS, Majzoub JA, Al-Zahrani A, Dallal GE, Blanco I and Roberts SB. High glycemic index foods, overeating , and obestiy. Pediatrics 1999; V 103, No. 3: E26.
- Marniemi J, Seppanen A, Hakala P. Long-term effects on lipid metabolism of weight reduction on lactovegetarian and mixed diet. Int J Obes 1990; V 14, No. 2: 113-125.
- McNutt, K. Fat traps, tips and tricks. Nutr Today 1992; May/June:47-49.
- National Institutes of Health: National Hear, Lung and Blood Institute. - Clinical guidelines on the identification, evaluation and treatment of overweight and obesity in adults. The Evidence Report. 1998.
National Institutes of Health: Weight-control Information Network, Web site: www.niddk.nig.gov/health/nutrit/win.htm
- Reaven GM Syndrome X. Clin Diab 1994; 12:32.
- Reaven GM. Do high carbohydrate diets prevent the development or attenuate the manifestations (or both) of syndrome X? a viewpoint stronly against. Curr Opin Lipidol 1997; 8(1): 23.
- Rolls BJ and Hill JO. Carbohydrates and Weight Management. International Life Sci-

ences Institute. ILSI Press, Washington DC, 1998.
- Sears B. Enter the Zone. Harper Collins, 1995. Steward HL, Morrison CB, Andrew SS, Balart LA. Sugar Busters. Ballantine Books, 1998.
- Tiwary CM, Ward JA, Jackson BA. Effect of pectin on satiety in healthy US Army adults. J Am Coll Nutr 1997; Vol 16 No. 5: 423-8.
- Toth MJ, Poehlman ET. Sympathetic nervous system activity and resting metabolic rate in vegetarians. Metabolism 1994; V 43, No. 5: 621-5.
- World Health Organization. The World Health Report 1998. Web site: http://www.who.int/whr/1998/whr- en.htm

Litterature used for the "Protein" chaptor:
- http://www.nealhendrickson.com/mcdougall/031200puprotein.htm
- McDougall J. The McDougall Plan. New Win Publ. 1983; pages 95-109.
- Leiter LA, Marliss EB. Survival during fasting may depend on fat as well as protein stores. JAMA 1982;248:2306
- Food and Nutrition Board, Institute of Medicine. Dietary Reference Intakes for Energy, Carbohydrate, Fiber, Fat, Fatty Acids, Cholesterol, Protein, and Amino Acids. Washington, DC: National Academy Press, 2002.
- Nutrition and athletic performance - Position of the American Dietetic Association, Dietitians of Canada, and the American College of Sports Medicine. J Am Diet Assoc 2000;100:1543-56.
- Messina V, Mangels R, Messina M. The Dietitian's Guide to Vegetarian Diets, 2nd ed. Sudbury, MA: Jones and Bartlett Publishers, 2004.
- Young VR, Pellett PL. Plant proteins in relation to human protein and amino acid nutrition. Am J Clin Nutr 1994;59 (suppl):1203S-1212S.
- Mangels AR, Messina V, Melina V. Position of The American Dietetic Association and Dietitians of Canada: Vegetarian diets. J Am Diet Assoc 2003;103:748-65
- Appleby, PN, Thoroughgood M, Mann, JI and Key T, The Oxford Study: an overview. Amer. J.Clin, Nutr, 1999 (suppl):525S-31S
- Ball D, Maughan RJ. Blood and urine acid-base status of premenopausal omnivorous and vegetarian women. British Journal of Nutrition. 1997;8(5):683-93.
- ESHA The Food Processor Nutritional Analysis Program
Messina M, Messina V, The Dietitians Guide to Vegetarian Diets: Issues and Applications, Chapter 3 and Appendix A. Gathersburg MD, Aspen Publishers; 1996
- Millward, J. Meat or wheat for the next millenium? The nutritional value of plant-based diets in relation to human amino acid and protein requirements. Proceedings

of the Nutrition Society 1999;58:249-260.
- Report of Joint FAO/WHO Expert Consultation, Protein Quality Evaluation, Food and Nutrition Paper 51, FAO of the United Nations, 1991
- Pennington, JA. Bowes and Church's Food Values of Portions Commonly Used. 16th ed. JB Lippincott Co, Philadelphia 1994.
- Protein in Vegetarian Diets. Vegetarian Health Letter, Loma Linda University, Loma Linda CA vegletter@sph.llu.edu 1998;1(7):1-3
- USDA Nutrient Database for Standard Reference at http://www.nal.usda.gov/fnic/cgi-bin/nut_search.pl

Litterature used for the "Older than adult" chaptor:
- American Dietetic Association Manual of Clinical Dietetics, Vegetarian Nutrition chapter, 2000 Baik H, and Russell R. B12 Deficiency In The Elderly. Annu. Rev. Nutr.. 19:357-377. 1999
- Carmel R, Cobalamin, the stomach, and aging. American Journal of Clinical Nutrition, 66:750-759, 1997.
- Carmel R, Green R, Jacobsen D, Rasmussen K, Florea M and Azen C, Serum cobalamin, homocysteine, and methylmalonic acid concentrations in a multiethnic elderly population: ethnic and sex differences in cobalamin and metabolite abnormalities. American Journal of Clinical Nutrition, Vol. 70, No. 5, 904-910.
- Houston D, Johnson M, Nozza R, Gunter E, Kelly J, Cutler G M, Edmonds J. Age-related hearing loss, vitamin B-12, and folate in elderly women. American Journal of Clinical Nutrition; 69(3) 564-571.
- Kort, W. Effect of aging. Nutrition Reviews. 58(3):S19-S21 Lichtenstein, A; Van Horn, L. Very Low Fat Diets, Circulation, Volume 98(9).September 1, 1998.935-939.
- Messina M, Messina V, The Dietitians Guide to Vegetarian Diets: Issues and Applications, Gathersburg MD, Aspen Publishers; 1996
- Papas A, Niessen L, Chauncey H. Geriatric Dentistry: Aging and Oral Health, Mosby Year Book,1991
- Potter S, Baum J, Teng H, Stillman R, Shay N and Erdman J, Soy protein and isoflavones: their effects on blood lipids and bone density in postmenopausal women. American Journal of Clinical Nutrition 68:1375S-1379S.
- Rosenburg IH. Nutrition in the elderly Nutr Rev:50;349-350, 1992
- Ryan C, Eleazer P, Egbert J. Vitamin D in the elderly. An overlooked nutrient. Nutrition Today. 1995;30:228- 233. 1995.
- Sciffman S, Moss J, Erickson R. Thresholds of food odors in the elderly. Exp Aging Res, 1976;2:389-398.

- Starling R, Ades P, Poehlman E. Physical activity, protein intake, and appendicular skeletal muscle mass in older men Am J Clin Nutr 1999;70:91-96.
- The Seventh-day Adventist Dietetic Association. Nutrition for Vegetarian/Vegan Seniors, pages 7-1 to 7-7 in
The Vegetarian/Vegan Resource (An Annex to Diet Manuals 1997-1998). Adventist Health. Roseville, CA. 1997.
- Ubbink J. Metabolic markers of vitamin nutritional status. American Journal of Clinical Nutrition, 70: 5, 789- 790, 1999.
- (Editorial) A Healthy Diet: The Fountain of Youth? Vegetarian Nutrition Health Letter, Loma Linda University, Loma Linda, CA. vegletter@sph.llu.edu 1999;2(8)1-4.
- Willett W. Convergence of philosophy and science: the third international congress on vegetarian nutrition. American Journal of Clinical Nutrition. 70(3 Suppl):434S-438S, 1999 Sep.
- Yates A, Schlicker S and Suitor C. Dietary Reference Intakes; The new basis for recommendations for calcium and related nutrients, B vitamins and choline. J. Amer. Diet. Assoc. 1998;98:(6):699-705.

Litterature used for the "Fat" chaptor:

- Anderson JW, Johnstone BM, Cook-Newell ME. Meta-analysis of the effects of soy protein intake on serum lipids. New Eng J Med 1995; Aug 3;333(5):276-82.
- Anderson JW, Zeigler JA, Deakins DA, Floore TL, Dillon DW, Wood CL, Oeltgen PR, Whitley RJ. Metabolic effects of high-carbohydrate, high-fiber diets for insulin-dependent diabetic individuals. Am J Clin Nutr 1991; Nov;54(5):936-43.
- Ågren J, Törmalä M, Nenonen M, Hänninen, O. Fatty acid composition of erythrocyte, platelet, and serum lipids in strict vegans. Lipids 1995; 30:365-369.
- American Dietetic Association. Position of the American Dietetic Association: Vegetarian Diets. JADA 1997; V 97, No. 11:1317-132.
Barnard RJ. Effects of life-style modification of serum lipids. Arch Intern Med 1991;151:1389-1394.
- Conquer JA. Dietary docosahexaenoic acid as a source of eicosapentaenoic acid in vegetarians and omnivores. Lipids 1997;32:341-345.
- Conquer JA, Holub BJ. Supplementation with an algae source of docosahexanoic acid increases (n-3) fatty acid status and alters selected risk factors for heart disease in vegetarian subjects. J Nutr 1996;126:3032-3039.
- Crane MG, Zielinski R, Aloia R. Cis and trans fats in omnivores, lacto-ovo vegetarians and vegans. Am J Clin Nutr 1988; 48:920 (abstr P2).
- Crawford MA costeloe K, Ghebremeskel K, Phylactos A, Skirvin L and Stacey F. Are

deficits of arachidonic and docosahexaenoic acids reponsible for the neural and vascular complications of preterm babies? Am J Clin Nutr 1997; Oct; 66(4 suppl): 1032S-1041S.
- Cunnane SC, Ganguli S, Menard C, Liede AC, Hamadeh MJ, Chen Z, Wolever TMS, Jenkins DJA. High alpha-linolenic acid flaxseed: some nutritional properties in humans. Br J Nutr 1993; 69:443-453.
- Dagnalie P, Van Staveren W. Macrobiotic nutrition and child health: results of a population-based, mixed- longtitudinal cohort study in the Netherlands. Am J Clin Nutr 1994;59(suppl):1187S-1196S.
- Draper A, Lewis J, Malhotra N, Wheeler E. The energy and nutrient intakes of different types of vegetarian: a case for supplements? [published erratum appears in Br J Nutr 1993 Nov;70(3):812]. Br J Nutr 1993; Jan;69(1):3-19.
- De Lorgeril M, Salen P, Martin JL, Monjaud I, Delaye J, Mamelle N. Mediterranean diet, traditional risk factors, and the rate of cardiovascular complications after myocardial infarction: final report of the Lyon Diet Heart Study. Circulation 1999; Feb. 16;99:779-785.
- De Lorgeril M, Salen MP, Delaye J. Effect of a Mediterranean type of diet on the rate of cardiovascular complications in patients with coronary artery disease. J Am Coll Cardiology 1996; 28(5):1103-8.
- D'Amico G, Gentile MG Manna G, Fellin G, Ciceri R, Cofano F, Petrini C, Lavarda F, Perolini S Porrini M. Effect of vegetarian soy diet on hyperlipidemia in nephrotic syndrome. Lancet. 1992; 339:1131-1134.
- Fraser GE, Linsted KD, Beeson WL. Effect of risk factor values on lifetime risk of and age at first coronary event: The Adventist Health Study. Am J Epidemiol 1995; 142:746-758.
- Gartner C, Stahl W, Sies H. Lycopene is more bioavailable from tomato paste than from fresh tomatoes. Am J Clin Nutr 1997;66:116-122.
- Giovannini M, Agostoni C and Salari PC. The role of lipids in nutrition during the first months of life. The Journal of International Medical Research 1991; 19: 351-362.
- Hachey DL. Benefits and risks of modifying maternal fat intake in pregnancy and lactation. Am J Clin Nutr 1994;59(suppl):454S-64S.
- Hoffman DR, Birch EE, Birch DG, Uauy R. Effects of w-3 long-chain polyunsaturated fatty acid supplementation on retinal and cortical development in premature infants. Am J Clin Nutr 1993; 57:807S-812S.
- Hoffman DR, Birch EE, Birch DG and Uauy R. Fatty acid profile of buccal cheek cell phospholipids as an index for dietary intake of docosahexaenoic acid in preterm infants. Lipids 1999; April 34(4): 337-42.

- Janelle KC, Barr SI. Nutrient intakes and eating behavior scores of vegetarian and nonvegetarian women. J Am Diet Assoc 1995; Feb;95(2):180-6, quiz 187-8.
- Jarvis K, Millre G. Fat in Infant Diets. Nutrition Today 1996; 31(5):182-191.
- Kanazawa T, Osanai T, Zhang XS, Uemura T, Yin XZ, Onodera K, Oike Y, Ohkubo, K. Protective effects of soy protein on the peroxidatizability of lipoproteins in cerebrovascular disease. J Nutr 1995; 125:639S-646S.

Kaplan R, Toshima M. Does a reduced fat diet cause retardation in child growth? Prev Med 1992; 21:33-52.
- Keys A, Menotti A, Toshima H. The diet and 15 –year death rate in the Seven Countries Study. Am J Epidemiol 1986; 124(6):903-15.
- Kies CV. Mineral utilization of vegetarians: impact of variation in fat intake. Am J Clin Nutr 1988; 48:884- 887.
- Krajcovicova-Kudlackova M, Simoncic R, Bederova A, Klvanova J. Plasma fatty acid profile and alternative nutrition. Ann Nutr Metab 1997; 41(6):365-70.
- Kushi LH, Folsom AR, Prineas RJ, Mink PJ, Bosick RM. Dietary antioxidant vitamins and death from coronary heart disease in postmenopausal women. N Engl J Med 1996; 334:1156-1162.
- McDougall J, Litzau K, Haver E, Saunders V, Spiller GA. Rapid reduction of serum cholesterol and blood pressure by a twelve-day, very low fat, strictly vegetarian diet. J Am Coll Nutr 1995; Oct;14(5):491-6.
- Melby CL, Foldflies DG and Toohey ML. Blood pressure differences in older black and white long-term vegetarians and nonvegetarians [published erratum appears in J Am Coll Nutr 1993; Dec;12(6):following table of contents]. J Am Coll Nutr 1993; June;12(3):262-9.
- Messina M, Erdman JW, eds. Second International Symposium on the role of soy in preventing and treating chronic disease. Am J Clin Nutr 1998; 68(6S):1329S-1515.
- Messina MJ, Messina VL. The Dietitian's Guide to Vegetarian Diets: Issues and Applications. Gaithersburg, MD: Aspen Publishers;1996.

Ornish D, Brown SE, Scherwitz LW, Billings JH, Armstrong WT, Ports TA, McLanahan SM, Kirkeeide RL, Brand RJ, Gould KL. Can lifestyle changes reverse coronary heart disease? The Lifestyle Heart Trial. Lancet 1990; Jul 21;336(8708):129-33.
- Ornish D, Scherwitz LW, Billings JH, Gould KL, Merritt TA, Sparler S, Armstrong WT, Ports TA, Kirkeeide RL, Hogeboom C, Brand RJ. Intensive lifestyle changes for reversal of coronary heart disease. JAMA 1998; Dec 16;280(23):2001-7.
- Rainey C, Nyquist L. Nuts – Nutrition and health benefits of daily use. Nutrition Today 1997; July/Aug;32(4);157-163.
- Sabaté J, Fraser GE, Burke K, Knutsen S, Bennett H, Lindsted KD. Effects of walnuts on

serum lipid levels and blood pressure in normal men. N Engl J Med 1993;328:603-607.
- Sanders TAB, Reddy S. The influence of a vegetarian diet on the fatty acid composition of human milk and the essential fatty acid status of the infant. Dept Nutr Dietetics 1992;120:S71-77.
- Sanders TA. Essential fatty acid requirements of vegetarians in pregnancy, lactation, and infancy. Am J Clin Nutr 1999; Sep;70(3 Suppl):555S-559S.
- Shinwell ED, Gorodischer R. Totally vegetarian diets and infant nutrition. Pediatrics 1982 Oct;70(4):582-6.
- Siguel, EN, Lerman RH. Altered fatty acid metabolism in patients with angiographically documented coronary artery disease. Metabolism 1994;43:982-993.
- Simopoulos AP. Essential fatty acids in health and chronic disease. Am J Clin Nutr 1999; Sep;70(3 Suppl):560S-569S.
- Simopoulos AP, Robinson J. The Omega Plan. New York NY: Harper Collins Publishers; 1998.
- Health and Welfare Canada. Nutrition Recommendations: The Report of the Scientific Review Committee. Ottawa ON: Supply and Services Canada; 1990.
- Sola R, Ville AE, Richard JL, Motta C, Bargallo MT, Girona J, Masana L, Jacotot B. Oleic acid rich diet protects against the oxidative modification of high density lipoproteins. Free Redic Biol Med 1997; 22(6):1037-
- Turley ML, Skeaff CM, Mann JI, Cox B. The effect of a low-fat, high-carbohydrate diet on serum high density lipoprotein cholesterol and triglyceride. Eur J Clin Nutr 1998; Oct;52(10):728-32.
- Uauy R, Peirano P, Hoffman D, Mena P, Birch D, Birch E. Role of essential fatty acids in the function of the developing nervous system. Lipids 1996; 31(suppl)167-176.
- Uauy R, Hoffman DR. Essential fat requirements of preterm infants. Am J Clin Nutr 2000; Jan;71(1 Suppl):245S-50S. Review.
- Vaisey-Genser M. Flaxseed: Health, Nutrition and Functionality. Winnipeg Canada: The flax council of Canada.
- Viola P. Olive Oil and Health. Spain: International Olive Oil Council; 1997.
- WHO Study Group on Diet, Nutrition and the Prevention of Non-communicable Diseases. Diet, Nutrition and the Prevention of Chronic Diseases. Geneva, Switzerland: Technical Report Series No. 797. World Health Organization, 1991.
- WHO and FAO Joint Consultation: Fats and Oils in Human Nutrition. Nutr Rev 1994;202-205.
- World Cancer Research Fund in Association with American Institute for Cancer Research. Food, Nutrition and the Prevention of Cancer: a Global Perspective. Menasha WI: Banta Book Group; 1997.
- Xiang M, Lei S, Li T, Zetterstrom R. Composition of long chain polyunsaturated fatty

acids in human milk and growth of young infants in rural areas of northern China. Acta Paediatr 1999; Feb;88(2):126-31.
- Zlotkin SH. A review of the Canadian "Nutrition Recommendations Update: Dietary Fat and Children". J Nut 1996; 126:1022S-1027.

Litterature used for the Growing up on plants chaptor:
- Acosta, P.B. Availability of essential amino acids and nitrogen in vegan diets. Am J Clin Nut 1988; 48: 868- 874.
- American Dietetic Association. Position of the American Dietetic Association: Vegetarian Diets. JADA 1997; V 97, No. 11:1317-132.
- Birch EE, Garfield S, Hoffman DR, Uauy R, Birch DG. A randomized controlled trial of early dietary supply of long-chain polyunsaturated fatty acids and mental development in term infants. Dev Med Child Neurol 2000 Mar;42(3):174-81.
- Borigato EVM, Martinez FE: Iron incorporation in Brazilian infant diets cooked in iron utensils. Nutrition Research 1992; 12: 1065-1073.
- Canadian Pediatric Society, Nutrition Committee. Position Statement. Meeting the iron needs of infants and young children: An update. Can. Med. Assoc. J. 1991; 144: 1451-1454.
- Carlson SE, Clandinin MT, Cook HW, Emken EA and Filer LJ Jr. trans Fatty acids: infant and fetal development. Am J Clin Nutr 1997; 66: 717S-36S.
- Crawford MA costeloe K, Ghebremeskel K, Phylactos A, Skirvin L and Stacey F. Are deficits of arachidonic and docosahexaenoic acids reponsible for the neural and vascular complications of preterm babies? Am J Clin Nutr 1997; Oct; 66(4 suppl): 1032S-1041S.
- Cunnane, SC, Francescutti V, Brenna, JT and Crawford, MA. Breast-fed infants achieve a higher rate of brain and whole body docosahexaenoate accumulation than formula-fed infants not consuming dietary docosahexaenoate. Lipids 2000, V 35, No. 1: 105-110.
- Dagnalie, P.C., Van Stavern, W.A. Vergote, F.J. et al. High prevalence of rickets in infants on macrobiotic diets. Am J Clin Nutr 1990; 51:202-208.
- Dwyer, J. T., Andrew, E. M., Berkey, M.A. et al. Growth in "new" vegetarian preschool children using the Jenss-Bayley curve fitting technique. Am J Clin Nutr 1983; 37: 815-827.
- Finley, D., Dewey, K., Lonnerdal, B. et al. 1985. Food choices of vegetarians and non-vegetarians during pregnancy and lactation. J. Am. Diet. Assoc. V.85 No. 6: 678-685.
- Gibson RS. Content and bioavailability of trace elements in vegetarian diets. Am J Clin Nut 1994; May;59(5 Suppl):1223S-1232S.

- Giovannini M, Agostoni C and Salari PC. The role of lipids in nutrition during the first months of life. The Journal of International Medical Research 1991; 19: 351-362.
- Glinsmann WH, Bartholmey SJ and Coletta F. Dietary guidelines for infants: a timely reminder. Nutrition Reviews 1996; V 54, No. 2: 50-57.
- Harper AE. Symposium: Dietary guidelines for children: a focus on fat. Dietary guidelines in perspective. American Institute of Nutrition. J Nutr 1996; 126: 1042S-1048S.
- Health and Welfare Canada. Nutrition in Pregnancy: National Guidelines. Minister of Supply and Services, 1986.
- Herbert, V. Vegetarianism. In: The Mount Sinai Complete Book of Nutrition, edited by Herbert, V. and Subak-Sharpe, G.J. New York: St. Martin's Press, 1990: 415-427.
- Hoffman DR, Birch EE, Birch DG and Uauy R. Fatty acid profile of buccal cheek cell phospholipids as an index for dietary intake of docosahexaenoic acid in preterm infants. Lipids 1999; April 34(4): 337-42.
Hornstra G. Essential fatty acids in mothers and their neonates. Am J Clin Nutr 2000 May;71(5 Suppl):1262S- 9S.
- Institute of Medicine Subcommittee on Nutritional Status and Weight Gain During Pregnancy: Nutrition During Pregnancy. Washington DC: National Academy Press, 1990.
- Institute of Medicine, Food and Nutrition Board. Dietary Reference Intakes for Thiamin, Riboflavin, Niacin, Vitamin B6, Folate, Vitamin B12, Pantothenic Acid, Biotin and Choline. Washington, DC: National Academy Press, 1998.
- Food and Nutrition Board. Recommended Dietary Allowances. 10th ed. Washington, DC: National Academy Press, 1989.
- Jacobs C, Dwyer JT. Vegetarian Children: Appropriate and inappropriate diets. Am J Clin Nutr 1988; 48 (suppl): 811-818.
- Kaplan RM and Toshima MT. Does a reduced fat diet cause retardation in child growth? Preventitive Medicine. 1992; 21: 33-52.
- Kleinman RE, Finberg LF, Klish WJ and Lauer RN. Symposium: Dietary guidelines for children: a focus on fat. Dietary guidelines for children: U. S. Recommendations. American Institute of Nutrition. J Nutr 1996; 126: 1028S-1030S.
- Lifshitz F and Tarim O. Symposium: Dietary guidelines for children: a focus on fat. Considerations about dietary fat restrictions for children. American Institute of Nutrition. J Nutr 1996; 126: 1031S-1041S.
- Mangels AR: 1991. Vegetarian infants and children: a review of recent research. Issues in Vegetarian Dietetics: Vol. 1 No. 2, 4-6.
- Mathias, B. Pass the Meat; The Growth of Vegetarian Teens. The Washington Post. D5, Aug. 25, 1992. Messina M, Messina V, The Dietitians Guide to Vegetarian Diets, Gathersburg MD, Aspen Publishers; 1996

- Miller GD. Symposium: Dietary guidelines for children: a focus on fat. American Institute of Nutrition. J Nutr 1996; 126: 1020S-1021S.
- Rolls, A and Walker, AF, editors. Nutrition and the Consumer: Issues in Nutrition and Toxicology. Vegetarianism: The Healthy Alternative? Elsevier Applied Science, New York, 1992.
- O'Connell, J.M, Dibley MJ, Sierra J et al. Growth of vegetarian children: The Farm Study. Pediatrics 1989; V.84, No. 3: 475-481.
- Sabate, J. Growth of lifetime vegetarian and non-vegetarian children 8 through 18 years. Presented at the Second International Congress on Vegetarian Nutrition. Arlington Virginia, 1992.
- Sabate J., Linstead, K.D. and Sanchez, A. 1991. Attained height of lacto-ovo vegetarian children and adults. Eur. J. Clin. Nutr. 45:51-58.
- Sanders, T.A.B. Growth and development of British vegan children. Am J Clin Nutr 1988;48:822-825.
- Sanders, T.A.B. and Reddy, S. 1992. The influence of a vegetarian diet on the fatty acid composition of human milk and the essential fatty acid status of the infant. J. Pediatr. V.120 No.4 P.2: S71-S76.
- Sanders TA. Essential fatty acid requirements of vegetarians in pregnancy, lactation, and infancy. Am J Clin Nutr 1999 Sep;70(3 Suppl):555S-559S.
- Shinwell, E.D. and Gorodischer, R. 1982. Totally vegetarian diets and infant nutrition. Pediatrics. 70:582-586.
- Specker B.L., Valanis B., Hertzberg V. et al. 1985. Sunshine exposure and serum 25-hydroxyvitamin D concentrations in exclusively breast-fed infants. J Pediatr. 107: 372-376.
- Suitor, C.W., Olson, C. and Wilson, J. 1993. Nutrition care during pregnancy and lactation: New guidelines from the Institute of Medicine. J. Am. Diet. Assoc. Vol. 93 No. 4: 478-479.
- Truesdell D.D., Acosta P.H. 1985. Feeding the vegan infant and child. J Amer. Diet. Assoc. 85: 837-840.
- Uauy R, Peirano P, Hoffman D, Mena P, Birch D, Birch E. Role of essential fatty acids in the function of the developing nervous system. Lipids 1996; 31(suppl)167-176.
- Uauy R, Hoffman DR. Essential fat requirements of preterm infants. Am J Clin Nutr 2000; Jan;71(1 Suppl):245S-50S. Review.
- Vieth R. Vitamin D supplementation, 25-hydroxyvitamin D concentrations, and safety. Am J Clin Nutr 1999;69:842–56.
- Xiang M, Lei S, Li T, Zetterstrom R. Composition of long chain polyunsaturated fatty acids in human milk and growth of young infants in rural areas of northern China. Acta Paediatr 1999; V. 88 No. 2:126-31.

Litterature for the Vitamins chaptor:
- The Vitamins. Gerald F. Combs Jr. Academic Press; 3 edition. 978-0121834937
- Abdulla M, Andersson I, Asp N, Berthelsen K, Birkhed D, Dencker I, Johansson C, Jagerstad M, Kolar K, Nair B, Nilsson-Ehle P, Norden A, Rassner A, Akesson B, and Ockerman P, Nutrient intake and health status of vegans. Chemical analyses of diets using the duplicate portion sampling technique Am J Clin Nutr 1981 34: 2464-2477.
- Groff J, Gropper S, Hunt S, Advanced nutrition and human metabolism, West Publ, 1995
- (Editorial) The Power of Antioxidants, Vegetarian Nutrition Health Letter, Loma Linda University, 2000; 3(3):1-4, (vegletter@sph.llu.edu)
- Haddad E, Berk L, Kettering J, Hubbard R, Peters W Dietary intake and biochemical, hematologic, and immune status of vegans compared with nonvegetarians Am J Clin Nutr 1999 70: 586S-593S.
- The Food Processor Nutritional Analysis Program, ESHA Research. http://www.esha.com/ Search for Antioxidant DRIs at http://www.nationalacademies.org/
- Yates A, Schlicker S and Suitor C. Dietary Reference Intakes; The new basis for recommendations for calcium and related nutrients, B vitamins and choline. J. Amer. Diet. Assoc. 1998;98:(6):699-705.
- Crane, M, Sample C, Patchett S, Register U, Vitamin B12 studies in total vegetarians (vegans). J. Nutr Med. 1994;4:419-430.
- Herbert V, Staging vitamin B-12 (cobalamin) status in vegetarians, American Journal of Clinical Nutrition, Vol 59, 1213S-1222S
Stabler SP, Lindenbaum J and Allen RH, Vitamin B-12 deficiency in the elderly: current dilemmas. American Journal of Clinical Nutrition, 66:741-749.
- Tucker K, Rich S, Rosenberg I, Jacques P, Dallal G, Wilson P, and Selhub, J. Plasma vitamin B-12 concentrations relate to intake source in the Framingham Offspring Study. Am J Clin Nutr 2000 71: 514-522.

Vitamin D
- Autier P, Severi G, Doré J, Boniol M. Has the sun protection factor had its day? BMJ 2000;320:1274 (6 May)
- Dawson-Hughes B, Dallal GE, Krall EA, Harris S, Sokoll LJ, Falconer G. Effect of vitamin D supplementation on wintertime and overall bone loss in healthy postmenopausal women. Ann Intern Med 1991; 115: 505-512.
- Jacques PF, Felson DT, Tucker KL, Mahnken B, Wilson PWF, Rosenberg IH, et al. Plasma 25-hydroxyvitamin D and its determinants in an elderly population sample. Am J Clin Nutr 1997; 66: 929-936
- Heaney, R, Lessons for nutritional science from vitamin D, American Journal of Clinical Nutrition, Vol. 69, No. 5, 825-826, May 1999

- W.F Loomis, Rickets in Human Nutrition, pp 193-203
- MacLaughlin J, Holick MF. Aging decreases the capacity of human skin to produce vitamin D3. J Clin Invest 1985;76:1536–8.
- McKenna MJ. Differences in vitamin D status between countries in young adults and the elderly. Am J Med 1992; 93: 69-77
- Messina M, Messina V, The Dietitians Guide to Vegetarian Diets: Issues and Applications, Chapter 3 and Appendix A. Gathersburg MD, Aspen Publishers; 1996
- Need AG, Morris HA, Horowitz M, Nordin B. Effects of skin thickness, age, body fat, and sunlight on serum 25-hydroxyvitamin D. Am J Clin Nutr 1993;58:882–5.
- Thomas MK, Lloyd-Jones DM, Thadhani RI, Shaw AC, Deraska DJ, Kitch BT, et al. Hypovitaminosis D in medical inpatients. N Engl J Med 1998; 338: 777-783
- Trang H, Cole D, Rubin LA, Pierratos A, Siu S, and Vieth R, Evidence that vitamin D3 increases serum 25- hydroxyvitamin D more efficiently than does vitamin D2 Am J Clin Nutr 1998 68: 854-858
- Vieth R. Vitamin D supplementation, 25-hydroxyvitamin D concentrations, and safety. Am J Clin Nutr 1999;69:842–56.

Litterature used for the "Babies, kids and young adults" chaptor:

- American Dietetic Association. Position of the American Dietetic Association: Vegetarian Diets. JADA 1997; V 97, No. 11:1317-132.
- Bronstrup A, Hages M, Prinz-Langenohl R and Pietrzik K. Effects of folic acid and combinations of folic acid and vitamin on plasma homocysteine concentrations in healthy, young women. Am J Clin Nutr 1998; Nov; 68(5): 1104-10.
- Carter JP, Furman T and Hutcheson HR Preeclampsia and reproductive performance in a community of vegans. Southern Med J 1987; 80:692-697.
- Conner W, Lowensohn, R and Hatcher L. Increased docosahexaenoic acid levels in human newborn infants by administration of sardines and fish oil during pregnancy. Lipids 1996; V 31(suppl)183S-187S.
- Dawson EB, Evans DR and Van Hook JW. Amniotic fluid B12 and folate levels associated with neural tube defects. Am J Perinatol 1998; 15(9): 511-4.
- Food and Nutrition Board. Recommended Dietary Allowances. 10th ed. Washington, DC: National Academy Press, 1989.
- Hachey DL. Benefits and risks of modifying maternal fat intake in pregnancy and lactation. Am J Clin Nutr 1994; 59(suppl): 454S-64S.
- Hambidge KM, Krebs NF, Sibley L et al. Acute effects of iron therapy on zinc status during pregnancy. Am J Clin Nutr 1996; 63: 884-90.
- Holman RT, Johnson SB and Ogburn PL. Deficiency of essential fatty acids and

membrane fluidity during pregnancy and lactation. Proc Natl Acad Sci USA 1991; V88: 4835-4839.
- Institute of Medicine Subcommittee on Nutritional Status and Weight Gain During Pregnancy: Nutrition During Pregnancy. Washington DC: National Academy Press, 1990.
- Institute of Medicine, Food and Nutrition Board. Dietary Reference Intakes for Thiamin, Riboflavin, Niacin, Vitamin B6, Folate, Vitamin B12, Pantothenic Acid, Biotin and Choline. Washington, DC: National Academy Press, 1998.
- Institute of Medicine, Food and Nutrition Board. Dietary Reference Intakes for Calcium, Phosphorus, Magnesium, Vitamin D and Fluoride. Washington DC: National Academy Press, 1997.
- Mangels, R. Vegetarian diets during pregnancy. Issues in Vegetarian Dietetics 1999; V 9 No. 1: 1, 4-8.
- Messina M, Messina V, The Dietitians Guide to Vegetarian Diets, Gathersburg MD, Aspen Publishers; 1996.
- Mills JL, Scott JM, Kirke PN, et al. Homocysteine and neural tube defects. Am J Epidemiol 2995; Vol 141, No. 7: 756S-760S.
- Prentice A. Maternal calcium requirements during preganacy and latations. Am J Clin Nutr 1994;59(suppl):477S-83S.
- Sanders T.A.B. and Reddy S. The influence of a vegetarian diet on the fatty acid composition of human milk and the essential fatty acid status of the infant. J. Pediatr. 1992V.120 No.4 P.2: S71-S76.
- Rush D. Periconceptional folate and neural tube defect. Am J Clin Nutr 1994; 59(suppl): 511S-6S.
- Scholl TO and Hediger ML. Anemia and iron-deficiency anemia: compliation of data on pregnancy outcome. Am J Clin Nutr 1994; 59(suppl): 492S-501S.
- Specker BL. Do North American women need supplemental vitamin D during pregnancy and lactation? Am J Clin Nutr 1994; 59(suppl): 484S-91S.
- Specker BL. Nutritional concerns of lactating women consuming vegetarian diets. Am J Clin Nutr 1994;59(suppl):1182S-6(S).
- Suitor, CW, Olson C and Wilson J. Nutrition care during pregnancy and lactation: New guidelines from the Institute of Medicine. J Am Diet Assoc 1993;V 93, No4: 478-479.
- Thomas J, Ellis FR. The health of vegans during pregnancy. Proc Nutr Soc 1977; 36;46A.
- Vander Put NM, Thomas CM, Eskes TK et al. Altered folate and vitamin B12 metabolism in families with spina-bifida offspring. QJM 1997; Aug; 90(8): 505-10.
- Acosta, P.B. Availability of essential amino acids and nitrogen in vegan diets. Am J

Clin Nut 1988; 48: 868- 874.
- American Dietetic Association. Position of the American Dietetic Association: Vegetarian Diets. JADA 1997; V 97, No. 11:1317-132.
- Birch EE, Garfield S, Hoffman DR, Uauy R, Birch DG. A randomized controlled trial of early dietary supply of long-chain polyunsaturated fatty acids and mental development in term infants. Dev Med Child Neurol 2000 Mar;42(3):174-81.
- Borigato EVM, Martinez FE: Iron incorporation in Brazilian infant diets cooked in iron utensils. Nutrition Research 1992; 12: 1065-1073.
- Canadian Pediatric Society, Nutrition Committee. Position Statement. Meeting the iron needs of infants and young children: An update. Can. Med. Assoc. J. 1991; 144: 1451-1454.
- Carlson SE, Clandinin MT, Cook HW, Emken EA and Filer LJ Jr. trans Fatty acids: infant and fetal development. Am J Clin Nutr 1997; 66: 717S-36S.
- Crawford MA costeloe K, Ghebremeskel K, Phylactos A, Skirvin L and Stacey F. Are deficits of arachidonic and docosahexaenoic acids reponsible for the neural and vascular complications of preterm babies? Am J Clin Nutr 1997; Oct; 66(4 suppl): 1032S-1041S.
- Cunnane, SC, Francescutti V, Brenna, JT and Crawford, MA. Breast-fed infants achieve a higher rate of brain and whole body docosahexaenoate accumulation than formula-fed infants not consuming dietary docosahexaenoate. Lipids 2000, V 35, No. 1: 105-110.
- Dagnalie, P.C., Van Stavern, W.A. Vergote, F.J. et al. High prevalence of rickets in infants on macrobiotic diets. Am J Clin Nutr 1990; 51:202-208.
- Dwyer, J. T., Andrew, E. M., Berkey, M.A. et al. Growth in "new" vegetarian preschool children using the Jenss-Bayley curve fitting technique. Am J Clin Nutr 1983; 37: 815-827.
- Finley, D., Dewey, K., Lonnerdal, B. et al. 1985. Food choices of vegetarians and non-vegetarians during pregnancy and lactation. J. Am. Diet. Assoc. V.85 No. 6: 678-685.
- Gibson RS. Content and bioavailability of trace elements in vegetarian diets. Am J Clin Nut 1994; May;59(5 Suppl):1223S-1232S.
- Giovannini M, Agostoni C and Salari PC. The role of lipids in nutrition during the first months of life. The Journal of International Medical Research 1991; 19: 351-362.
- Glinsmann WH, Bartholmey SJ and Coletta F. Dietary guidelines for infants: a timely reminder. Nutrition Reviews 1996; V 54, No. 2: 50-57.
- Harper AE. Symposium: Dietary guidelines for children: a focus on fat. Dietary guidelines in perspective. American Institute of Nutrition. J Nutr 1996; 126: 1042S-1048S.
- Health and Welfare Canada. Nutrition in Pregnancy: National Guidelines. Minister of Supply and Services, 1986.

- Herbert, V. Vegetarianism. In: The Mount Sinai Complete Book of Nutrition, edited by Herbert, V. and Subak-Sharpe, G.J. New York: St. Martin's Press, 1990: 415-427.
- Hoffman DR, Birch EE, Birch DG and Uauy R. Fatty acid profile of buccal cheek cell phospholipids as an index for dietary intake of docosahexaenoic acid in preterm infants. Lipids 1999; April 34(4): 337-42.
- Hornstra G. Essential fatty acids in mothers and their neonates. Am J Clin Nutr 2000 May;71(5 Suppl):1262S- 9S.
- Institute of Medicine Subcommittee on Nutritional Status and Weight Gain During Pregnancy: Nutrition During Pregnancy. Washington DC: National Academy Press, 1990.
- Institute of Medicine, Food and Nutrition Board. Dietary Reference Intakes for Thiamin, Riboflavin, Niacin, Vitamin B6, Folate, Vitamin B12, Pantothenic Acid, Biotin and Choline. Washington, DC: National Academy Press, 1998.Food and Nutrition Board. Recommended Dietary Allowances. 10th ed. Washington, DC: National Academy Press, 1989.
- Jacobs C, Dwyer JT. Vegetarian Children: Appropriate and inappropriate diets. Am J Clin Nutr 1988; 48 (suppl): 811-818.
- Kaplan RM and Toshima MT. Does a reduced fat diet cause retardation in child growth? Preventitive Medicine. 1992; 21: 33-52.
- Kleinman RE, Finberg LF, Klish WJ and Lauer RN. Symposium: Dietary guidelines for children: a focus on fat. Dietary guidelines for children: U. S. Recommendations. American Institute of Nutrition. J Nutr 1996; 126: 1028S-1030S.
- Lifshitz F and Tarim O. Symposium: Dietary guidelines for children: a focus on fat. Considerations about dietary fat restrictions for children. American Institute of Nutrition. J Nutr 1996; 126: 1031S-1041S.
- Mangels AR: 1991. Vegetarian infants and children: a review of recent research. Issues in Vegetarian Dietetics: Vol. 1 No. 2, 4-6.
- Mathias, B. Pass the Meat; The Growth of Vegetarian Teens. The Washington Post. D5, Aug. 25, 1992.
- Messina M, Messina V, The Dietitians Guide to Vegetarian Diets, Gathersburg MD, Aspen Publishers; 1996
- Miller GD. Symposium: Dietary guidelines for children: a focus on fat. American Institute of Nutrition. J Nutr 1996; 126: 1020S-1021S.
- Rolls, A and Walker, AF, editors. Nutrition and the Consumer: Issues in Nutrition and Toxicology. Vegetarianism: The Healthy Alternative? Elsevier Applied Science, New York, 1992.
- O'Connell, J.M, Dibley MJ, Sierra J et al. Growth of vegetarian children: The Farm Study. Pediatrics 1989; V.84, No. 3: 475-481.

- Sabate, J. Growth of lifetime vegetarian and non-vegetarian children 8 through 18 years. Presented at the Second International Congress on Vegetarian Nutrition. Arlington Virginia, 1992.
- Sabate J., Linstead, K.D. and Sanchez, A. 1991. Attained height of lacto-ovo vegetarian children and adults. Eur. J. Clin. Nutr. 45:51-58.
- Sanders, T.A.B. Growth and development of British vegan children. Am J Clin Nutr 1988;48:822-825.
- Sanders, T.A.B. and Reddy, S. 1992. The influence of a vegetarian diet on the fatty acid composition of human milk and the essential fatty acid status of the infant. J. Pediatr. V.120 No.4 P.2: S71-S76.
- Sanders TA. Essential fatty acid requirements of vegetarians in pregnancy, lactation, and infancy. Am J Clin Nutr 1999 Sep;70(3 Suppl):555S-559S.
- Shinwell, E.D. and Gorodischer, R. 1982. Totally vegetarian diets and infant nutrition. Pediatrics. 70:582- 586.
- Specker B.L., Valanis B., Hertzberg V. et al. 1985. Sunshine exposure and serum 25-hydroxyvitamin D concentrations in exclusively breast-fed infants. J Pediatr. 107: 372-376.
- Suitor, C.W., Olson, C. and Wilson, J. 1993. Nutrition care during pregnancy and lactation: New guidelines from the Institute of Medicine. J. Am. Diet. Assoc. Vol. 93 No. 4: 478-479.
- Truesdell D.D., Acosta P.H. 1985. Feeding the vegan infant and child. J Amer. Diet. Assoc. 85: 837-840.
- Uauy R, Peirano P, Hoffman D, Mena P, Birch D, Birch E. Role of essential fatty acids in the function of the developing nervous system. Lipids 1996; 31(suppl)167-176.
- Uauy R, Hoffman DR. Essential fat requirements of preterm infants. Am J Clin Nutr 2000; Jan;71(1 Suppl):245S-50S. Review.
- Vieth R. Vitamin D supplementation, 25-hydroxyvitamin D concentrations, and safety. Am J Clin Nutr 1999;69:842–56
- Xiang M, Lei S, Li T, Zetterstrom R. Composition of long chain polyunsaturated fatty acids in human milk and growth of young infants in rural areas of northern China. Acta Paediatr 1999; V. 88 No. 2:126-31.

CPSIA information can be obtained at www.ICGtesting.com
Printed in the USA
BVOW020802270912

301558BV00001B/8/P